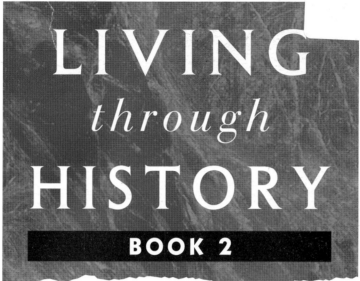

LIVING
through
HISTORY
BOOK 2

Foundation Edition

the Making of the
United Kingdom
and
Black Peoples
of the Americas

Fiona Reynoldson
and
David Taylor

CONTENTS

Black Peoples of the Americas

It was difficult being a king or queen. Other people wanted to be powerful too.

In 1485 Henry VII defeated Richard III at the Battle of Bosworth Field. Henry VII became the first Tudor king.

The Tudor kings and queens

- Henry VII
- Henry VIII
- Edward VI
- Mary
- Elizabeth I

End of the Tudors

Elizabeth I had no children. So her cousin became king when she died. He was called James Stuart.

The Stuart kings and queens

- James I (James Stuart)
- Charles I
- Parliament ruled
- Charles II
- James II
- William and Mary
- Anne.

Parliament

Parliament was made up of several hundred rich men. They were called **Members of Parliament (MPs)**. They met to talk. They talked about what the king or queen should do.

Sometimes they said he or she should go to war. Other times they said that too much money was spent by the king or queen.

What Members of Parliament wanted

Most of all the Members of Parliament wanted the king or queen to listen to what they said. Quite often this annoyed kings like Charles I.

Source B

Henry VIII.

Source A

King Henry VIII talking to a diplomat from Venice. He was trying to see if he looked more manly than his rival, the King of France.

His majesty asked 'Is the King of France as tall as I am?'

I replied 'He is about the same'.

He then asked 'Is he fat?'

I answered 'No he isn't'.

Henry finally asked 'Does he have strong legs? Look at my legs. Aren't they the legs of a fit and athletic man?'.

Source C

James II.

Everyday life

Most people lived by farming. They kept cows, sheep and other animals. They grew wheat and vegetables. Very rich people had servants to farm for them.

A few people worked as merchants. They bought and sold things like leather, wine and cloth. A very few people sailed to discover new lands. Some made lots of money by bringing back all sorts of spices and gold and silver to sell.

The king or queen, together with the Church, were very powerful. (Although sometimes it was more like arm wrestling.)

The rows got so bad that King Charles I went to war against Parliament. Parliament won. And Parliament chopped the king's head off.

Religion

Religion was very important. Almost everyone believed in God. The Church was God's power on Earth. So almost everyone did what the Church said.

Changes in religion

Henry VII became king in 1485. Everyone was a **Catholic**. Then after Henry VIII, most people became **Protestant**. There were lots of arguments about religion all through the Tudors and Stuarts.

Questions

1 Who was the first Tudor king?

2 Who was the first Stuart king?

3 What did Parliament do to Charles I?

4 When Henry VII became king everyone was Catholic. What religion did most people become after Henry VIII?

5 How did most people make their living at this time?

6 What can we learn about Henry VIII from Source A?

Choosing religion or not

There are many different religions in Britain today.

Religion in Tudor times

In early Tudor times there was only one religion in Britain – Christianity. And every Christian was in the Catholic Church. It was the only Church. It was headed by the **Pope**. He lived far away in Rome.

The church in the village

The church building was large. It was often in the middle of the village. Everyone went to church on Sunday to pray and think about God. At other times there were dances and feasts in the main part of the church.

Pictures in the church

There were lots of pictures in the church. Some were painted on the walls. Some were in glass in windows. The pictures showed good people who loved God. They also showed what happened to bad people. They went to Hell.

The Church became rich

Some people said that the Church had become too rich. It was too powerful. They said that some bishops and priests were lazy or wanted money. They were no longer good people at all. They did not follow the way of Jesus Christ.

The Pope

The Pope was the head of the Church. Some people said that Popes were not always good men. They liked money. Some Popes sold jobs in the Church to rich men.

Other people said that the Pope was a foreigner. He should not tell people in England what to do.

Source A

A report on a monastery in 1535.

Many of the monks devote themselves to hunting and shooting arrows.

The abbot is often drunk.

Some of the monks spend their time gambling with dice.

This church window shows Hell as the mouth of a monster.

Source B

The Reformation

Many people all over Europe wanted to reform or change the Church. They wanted the Church to be more simple and pure. One of these reformers was Luther, who lived in Germany.

Several other countries had a Reformation. They changed their Church and became Protestant.

The Reformation in England

Under Henry VIII, England changed religion from Catholic to Protestant.

How the Church was organised in early Tudor times

The picture below shows how the Church was organised in early Tudor times. Later, Henry VIII got rid of abbots, priors, monks, nuns and the Pope.

Questions

1 What was the only religion in early Tudor times?

2 a Who was head of the Catholic Church?
  b What complaints did people have about this person?

3 Write down four reasons why people went to the church in the village.

4 Look at Source B. What does the picture show?

5 Why do you think the men who ran the Church wanted pictures like this in churches?

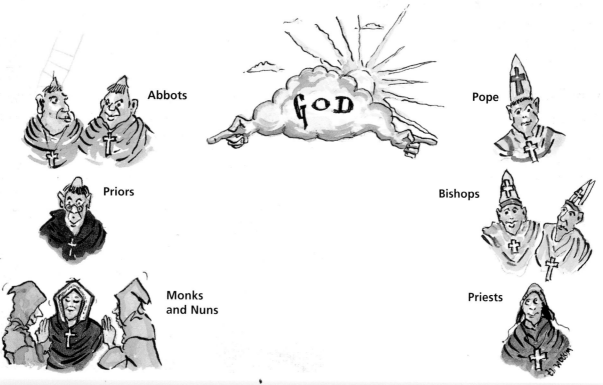

How the Church was organised in Tudor times.

1.3 HENRY VIII AND THE BREAK WITH THE POPE

Henry VIII

Henry VII died in 1509. His son, Henry VIII, became king. Henry VIII married Catherine of Aragon. They were happily married.

Henry and religion

Henry was religious. He supported the Catholic Church. He also supported the Pope, who was head of the Catholic Church.

Henry needed a son

Henry said he must have a son to be king after him. If he had a daughter, she would not be strong enough to control England.

Anne Boleyn.

I must have a son!

Only a daughter

It was 1527. Henry and Catherine had been married for many years. But they only had one daughter. Her name was Mary. Henry was desperate for a son. Catherine was too old to have any more children. So Henry said he must have a divorce from her.

Henry and the divorce

Henry asked the Pope for a divorce from Catherine. But the Pope was in a difficult position. He was being held prisoner by Catherine's nephew, Emperor Charles V. Charles V was angry and told the Pope to say 'no' to the divorce. Henry was furious.

Henry in love

Meanwhile, Henry had fallen in love with Anne Boleyn. She became pregnant in 1533. All the astrologers told Henry it would be a boy. Now Henry had to marry Anne quickly. But how could he get rid of Catherine?

Henry went against the Pope

The Pope would not give Henry a divorce. So Henry decided to go against the Pope. The leading churchman in the country was Thomas Cranmer. He was the Archbishop of Canterbury. Henry told Cranmer to let him have a divorce.

The divorce

Cranmer, as Archbishop of Canterbury, gave Henry a divorce from his wife, Catherine of Aragon.

Henry and Anne

Then Henry married Anne Boleyn. He waited for his baby to be born. Everyone was sure it would be a son. But it was a daughter. She was called Elizabeth.

Henry was bitterly disappointed.

Henry's six wives, his reasons for marrying them, and how the marriages ended.

Questions

1 Who was Henry VIII married to for many years?

2 Why didn't Henry want a daughter?

3 What was the name of Henry and Anne's daughter?

Source C

A foreign visitor describes Anne Boleyn.

Anne has a brown face, long neck and wide mouth.

She has the king's affection.

Her eyes are big and black.

She has black hair which she wears loose.

The end of Anne Boleyn

Anne had another baby. But it died. She had no more living children. So that was the end of Anne. Henry said she was a witch and had many lovers. Then he had her head chopped off.

Henry married again. This time he had a son (Edward). But what was Henry going to do about his row with the Pope?

Henry as Supreme Head of the Church

Henry wanted to be head of the Church, instead of the Pope. The Members of Parliament also wanted to be free of the Pope. So Parliament said it would make Henry the Supreme Head of the Church in England.

Now Henry was in charge of the Church. He was pleased.

Henry and Thomas More

Thomas More was an important Catholic. He said that Henry was wrong. He must not go against the Pope and the Catholic Church. But Henry had Thomas More executed.

Henry and the monasteries

Many people said the monasteries were not good and holy any more. Also, the monasteries had lots of money and land.

Henry had started to attack the Church because it had made it so difficult to divorce Catherine of Aragon. It was very easy for him to go on attacking the Church. He wanted the monasteries and land.

Source D

A picture from the time, showing Henry trampling on the Pope.

Questions

1 What did Parliament say it would make Henry?

2 a Who was Thomas More?
   b What happened to him?

3 How many monasteries were there in England and Wales?

4 What was the dissolution of the monasteries?

Henry and Thomas Cromwell

Henry made Thomas Cromwell his chief inspector. Together they sent men to inspect all 850 monasteries in England and Wales.

The men found that the 850 monasteries owned about a quarter of all the land in the country. They had lots of gold and silver too. The men also found that some monasteries did not do good work any more.

The dissolution of the monasteries, 1535–1539

Henry closed the monasteries. This was called the **dissolution of the monasteries**. Henry also shut down the nunneries, where nuns lived and worked. Henry sold their land and kept the money. Then he spent the money on wars.

A modern artist's impression of the scene where a nunnery was closed down.

What was Fountains Abbey?

Fountains Abbey was a big abbey in Yorkshire. It was very rich.

Many monks lived and worked in Fountains Abbey.

Source A

Fountains Abbey.

The story of Fountains Abbey

1132	The abbey was started.
1150–1200	Rich people gave money and land to the abbey.
	The monks farmed sheep and mined lead and iron.
1200–1265	The abbey became rich.
1300–1399	The monks ate meat very often.
	They paid servants to farm the land.
1536	The Abbot resigned.
	Marmaduke Bradley paid to become Abbot.
1539	The monks surrendered to the king.
1540	The abbey was stripped of its treasures and sold.

Rules at Fountains Abbey

The monks at Fountains lived by strict rules.

1 Monks had to:

- pray
- work (on the farm)
- study
- help the poor
- teach
- look after travellers.

2 Monks had to live far from a town.

3 Monks had to live from their farming.

4 Monks did not usually eat meat.

Source B

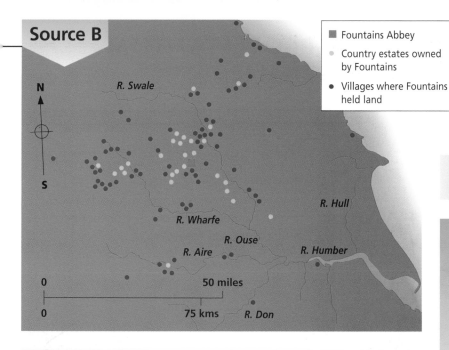

Legend:
- ■ Fountains Abbey
- ○ Country estates owned by Fountains
- ● Villages where Fountains held land

N
S

R. Swale

R. Hull

R. Wharfe

R. Ouse

R. Aire

R. Humber

0 — 50 miles

0 — 75 kms — R. Don

Land owned by Fountains Abbey.

Source D

Robert Aske said that Henry VIII was wrong to close the monasteries.

The abbeys and monasteries gave money and food to poor people. They were beautiful places where men and women could serve God.

Source C

A report from an inspector of monasteries. It was sent to Thomas Cromwell in 1536.

The Abbot of Fountains Abbey has ruined the abbey, wasting his woodland and keeping six mistresses. He stole an emerald and a ruby from a gold cross. He has resigned.

There is a monk at the abbey called Marmaduke. He is wise. He will pay 600 marks (£400) to be made abbot.

Questions

1 Where was Fountains Abbey?

2 Read the **Rules of Fountains Abbey**.

Write out what the monks had to do.

3 Read Source C.

a What had the abbot done?

b Do you think that everything in the report was true? Give one reason why you might not believe the report.

4 Read Source D.

Robert Aske wanted the monasteries to stay open. Write down the two reasons he gave.

5 Read **The Story of Fountains Abbey**.

a When was the abbey started?

b When did the monks surrender to the King?

c When was the abbey stripped of its treasures?

Edward VI became king

Henry VIII died in 1547.

The new king was his son, Edward. Edward was only nine years old.

Would England be Protestant or Catholic?

Henry had broken with the Pope. But he still had Catholic services in the churches. Many people wanted to go further. They wanted to be full Protestants (see the box on page 15).

Edward and the Duke of Northumberland

Edward was so young that a powerful man ruled for him. This man was called the Duke of Northumberland. The Duke was a Protestant. So he made England even more Protestant.

Edward VI fell ill

Edward fell ill with tuberculosis.

The Duke of Northumberland was very worried. If Edward died, Edward's sister Mary would be queen. Mary was a very strong Catholic.

Source A

The death of Lady Jane Grey.

The executioner gave her a handkerchief to tie round her eyes. He knelt and asked her to forgive him, which she did. She lay her head on the block and prayed.

Questions

1 When did Henry VIII die?

2 How old was Edward VI when he became king?

3 Which Duke controlled Edward VI?

4 What religion was this Duke?

5 What religion was Mary?

6 Why was Lady Jane Grey executed?

How England became Protestant under Edward VI

1547 Protestant books had to be read in all churches.

1548 All statues and paintings were taken from churches.

1549 All churches had to use the new Protestant prayer book. It was written by Archbishop Cranmer. Priests had to wear plain clothes.

A painting of the execution of Lady Jane Grey. It was painted in the nineteenth century.

The Duke of Northumberland's plot

The Duke of Northumberland had a plot. His daughter-in-law, Lady Jane Grey, was Henry VIII's niece. The Duke would make her queen.

Edward was dying. He agreed that Lady Jane Grey should be queen. But many powerful people did not like this. They thought that Mary was the rightful queen. After all, Mary was Henry VIII's daughter.

Mary became queen

The Duke of Northumberland was captured and beheaded. Mary became queen in 1553. England became Catholic again.

Soon after, Mary was worried that Lady Jane Grey might try to become queen. So Mary had Lady Jane beheaded.

Some differences between Catholics and Protestants

Catholic	Protestant
Church services were in Latin.	Church services were in English.
The Pope was head of the Church.	A king could be head of the Church.
What the Church said was true.	Only what the Bible said was true.
Churches should have statues and paintings.	Churches should be plain.
Priests wore colourful clothes.	Priests wore plain clothes.

Mary became queen

Mary became queen in 1553. England was used to having kings rule the country. A queen was a nice change from a king. Many people were pleased.

Mary and religion

But people were not pleased that Mary was a Catholic. She wanted everyone to be Catholic.

Bloody Mary

Mary had Protestants put to death. It was not long before people called her Bloody Mary.

What Mary did for Catholics

1 Catholic church services came back.

2 Protestant priests lost their jobs.

3 Mary tried to re-open monasteries.

   However, most of the land had been sold.

4 Mary married King Philip of Spain.

   Spain was a Catholic country.

5 In 1555 Mary had some important Protestants burnt to death. This was unpopular with many people. They felt it was very brutal.

Mary's life

Mary was born in 1516. Her mother was Catherine of Aragon. Her father was Henry VIII.

Henry divorced Catherine when Mary was eleven years old.

After her half brother Edward died, Mary became queen.

She had a younger half sister called Elizabeth.

Source A

From a diary at the time.

Mary became queen of England in July 1553. The bells rang out. There were bonfires and feasts in every street.

Source B

The burning of Thomas Cranmer in 1556. This was painted in the nineteenth century.

Another picture showing the burning of Thomas Cranmer. This picture is in a best selling book from the time.

Source D

One Protestant bishop comforted another. They were both about to be burnt.

We shall this day light such a candle by God's grace in England as I shall trust shall never be put out.

Source E

This was written two days after Cranmer's burning. Before he was burnt, Cranmer had signed some papers saying that he gave up being a Protestant. Just before he died he went back on this.

Cranmer put out his right hand into the flame and held it there until his hand was seen on fire. He cried out 'This hand has done wrong.'

Source F

From a diary in 1558.

Queen Mary died. All the churches in London rang their bells.

That night bonfires were lit and tables put in the streets for eating and drinking.

Questions

1 When did Mary become queen?

2 Why were many people pleased about Mary being queen?

3 What did Mary do to some Protestants?

4 Read **Mary's life**.

 a Write down the names of Mary's half brother and half sister.

 b Look at the drawing of Henry VIII's six wives on page 9. Write down the names of his first three wives. These were the mothers of his three children.

5 Read Source A.

 What things happened to celebrate when Mary became queen?

6 Read Source F.

 Why do you think Mary was unpopular by the time she died?

Elizabeth I was the daughter of Henry VIII and Anne Boleyn.

Elizabeth was a Protestant. But she was not strongly against the Catholics. She wanted a middle way.

Trouble with Catholics

A middle way was difficult. In 1569 some Catholics wanted England to be fully Catholic again. Elizabeth had the leaders executed. All seemed well. Then in 1570, the Pope said that Elizabeth was a wicked woman. All Catholics must rebel against her. They must get rid of her.

Support for Elizabeth

Lots of English people were angry. The Pope was a foreigner. They did not want him telling them what to do. They supported Elizabeth.

The law and Catholics

People said the law against Catholics must be harder. They did not want foreign Catholic priests coming to England.

Catholic priests had to hide in special **priestholes** (secret rooms) in Catholic people's houses. You can see one of these in Source B.

Trouble from Puritans

Puritans did not like Catholics. They wanted the Church to be even more Protestant than it was. They did not like the middle way. Puritans wanted the Church to be pure and simple (see the picture at top of page 19). They believed that everything must be plain.

Source A

What the Pope said in 1570.

Elizabeth, the pretended Queen of England, has said she is the Supreme Head of the Church in England.

We command everyone not to obey her.

What Queen Elizabeth said

I am Head of the Church.

Everyone must go to church or pay a fine.

Everyone must use the Protestant prayer book.

Catholic priests lose their jobs but none will be killed.

Priests can wear coloured clothes.

No music, statues or stained glass windows. No brightly coloured clothing, dancing, theatres or drinking to excess.

We want: long sermons based on the Bible, a God-fearing life, more schools and colleges, help for the poor.

What Puritans believed.

Source B

A priesthole.

Spain and England in the 1580s

Elizabeth was more worried about Spain than about the Puritans. The King of Spain was a strong Catholic. He agreed with the Pope. He wanted to get rid of Elizabeth and make England Catholic again.

The Spanish Armada, 1588

The Spanish sent a great fleet of ships to fight England. It was called the Spanish Armada. The English followed the Spanish up the English Channel. Then they fought and at last, a storm hit the ships.

The Spanish ships were blown north. Many were wrecked. Only half the ships got back to Spain. The danger to Elizabeth was over.

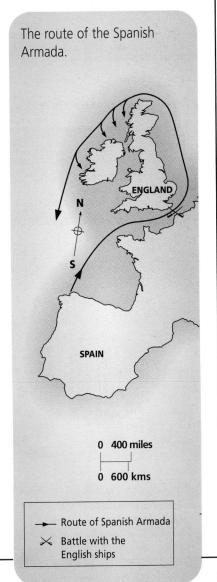

The route of the Spanish Armada.

ENGLAND

N

S

SPAIN

0   400 miles

0   600 kms

→ Route of Spanish Armada

✕ Battle with the English ships

Questions

1 Who was Elizabeth I?

2 What religion was Elizabeth I?

3 Look at the picture about what Puritans believed on this page.

   a What did Puritans **not** want?
   b What did Puritans want?

4 When was the Spanish Armada?

5 What happened to the Spanish ships called the Armada?

Thomas Kytson – a rich merchant

Thomas Kytson was a rich **merchant**. He made a lot of money, buying and selling woollen cloth.

He built a beautiful, big house at Hengrave in Suffolk. It had a vineyard, fish ponds and gardens.

Thomas Kytson died in 1540. He left Hengrave to his widow. She was expecting a baby. The baby was a son. This was young Thomas Kytson.

Young Thomas Kytson gets married

When young Thomas Kytson grew up, he married Jane Paget. But she died within a year.

Young Thomas Kytson gets married again

Next he married Elizabeth Cornwallis. She came from a strong Catholic background. Young Thomas was also a Catholic. At first, young Thomas was not very careful about religion. He easily fell out with Elizabeth I (see Sources C and D).

Queen Elizabeth's visit in 1578

By 1578, young Thomas was in favour. Elizabeth visited him at Hengrave. She made him a knight (Sir Thomas Kytson).

Elizabeth's visit cost him a lot of money. He gave huge feasts for her and all her followers. He also gave her presents and put on shows.

Source A

Hengrave Hall as it is today.

A fashionable Tudor gentleman.

The end of young Thomas – 1602

Thomas stayed a Catholic all his life. As long as he was not too open about it, Elizabeth did not mind. But there were times when he went too far. Both he and his wife spent some time in prison for being too open about their Catholic beliefs. But Elizabeth did not take away their possessions.

When Thomas died in 1602, he was still a very rich man.

Source B

The Kytson coat of arms.

Source C

A letter from young Thomas Kytson.

I understand I am accused of saying that the Queen does not care about religion.

I have never thought it and therefore certainly never said it.

I have been most unfairly slandered.

I beg you not to think badly of me.

Source D

A letter from young Thomas Kytson to Queen Elizabeth when she was first queen. He did not keep his promises.

I have been in prison since last September.

What I said then about religion was because I did not understand.

Now I want to obey the laws on religion. I will not be lazy in listening to sermons, reading books on religion and listening to wise men talk about religion.

Life at Hengrave

The Kytsons were rich. Elizabeth Kytson was in charge of running the house. This was a big job. She had servants to clean the house and do the washing. She had at least two cooks and other kitchen servants to make the meals.

Food

There was no running down to the shops to buy food. Most food was grown on the farm at home. A lot of food had to be stored so that it could be eaten in the winter time.

Food easily goes bad. There were no freezers or tins. Food had to be salted, dried, pickled and so on.

How food was stored

- Flour was made from wheat grown on the farm. The flour was stored in big, wooden tubs. It was used to make bread.

- Meat was salted in barrels.

- Vegetables were pickled.

- Fruit was preserved, often in sugar.

- Honey was collected from beehives.

- Herbs were dried.

Farm work

Women servants usually milked the cows, and made butter and cheese. They also looked after the hens.

Source E

From the account books at Hengrave.

Sums of money have to be paid for:

- books for Margaret and Mary

- making silk dresses

- a bear man for bringing his bears to perform

- money lost in gambling by the master.

Source F

LADY KYTSON

Elizabeth Kytson. She was a strong person. Her father asked her to sort out family quarrels.

The tomb of Thomas and Elizabeth Kytson in the local Protestant church.

The first wife of Thomas Kytson, Jane Paget, is also on the tomb. But notice how she has been pushed into the corner.

Farming the land

There was a lot of land at Hengrave. Many farm workers worked in the fields, the gardens and the vineyard. There were also men to look after the horses and other animals, ponds and gardens.

Entertainment

The Kytsons were rich. They had lots of people to visit. They feasted and they entertained. Music was very popular – the Kytsons kept a band of musicians at Hengrave Hall all the time.

Source H

Elizabeth Kytson helped the poor.

From 1625 Elizabeth gave £30 a year for houses for the poor.

From 1626 she gave £4 a year for new clothes for twelve poor people.

Questions

1 Where was most of the Kytsons' food grown?

2 How was meat stored?

3 Read Source E.

   Name two sorts of entertainment apart from music.

4 The Kytsons were always Catholics. Look at Source H. How does this show that they kept in with the Protestant religion?

5 Why do you think the statue of Jane Paget on the tomb in Source G has been pushed into the corner?

Parliament today

Parliament is made up of:

- the House of Commons (nearly 700 Members of Parliament)
- the House of Lords
- the Queen.

The **House of Commons** is the most powerful part of Parliament. It makes the laws. It also agrees how much money is given in taxes by ordinary people.

The **House of Lords** gives advice and agrees the laws.

The Queen signs the laws.

Voting

Nearly everyone who is over eighteen years old votes for a Member of Parliament. When people vote it is called a **general election**.

Tudor parliaments

Parliament was made up of the king or queen, the House of Lords and the House of Commons (about 300 Members of Parliament).

The king or queen ran the country. There were twenty or thirty rich, powerful lords who helped. The king or queen only asked the House of Commons to meet when they had to. That was usually when the king or queen needed more money to fight a war. Also, only the whole of Parliament together could pass new laws.

How Parliament could get more powerful.

Source A

Parliament in the 1990s.

Parliament under Henry VII

Parliament was not powerful under Henry VII.

Henry was a careful king. He did not want new laws and he did not want to fight wars.

Henry just wanted to rule as king.

Henry hardly ever called Parliament to meet.

Parliament under Henry VIII

Henry VIII was quite different to Henry VII. He wanted to pass laws to change religion. He also wanted to fight wars.

Henry kept calling Parliament to meet. The 300 Members of Parliament came to London for weeks on end. Often they wanted to go home. But changing England's religion was important. They passed law after law.

Source B

Henry VIII sitting at the head of Parliament.

Questions

1 How many Members of Parliament are there in the House of Commons today?

2 How many Members of Parliament were there in the House of Commons in Tudor times?

3 Give two reasons why Tudor kings and queens had to call parliaments.

Edward and Mary

Both Edward and Mary had to call Parliament

1 to pass laws, and

2 to give money.

Elizabeth had to call Parliament when she became queen for the same reasons.

Elizabeth I and Parliament

For most of the time, Elizabeth lived on her own money. She had about £200,000 a year. The money came from rent (she owned a lot of land), customs duties and so on. But sometimes Elizabeth needed more money:

- She needed money for war against Spain.

- She needed money to pay for ships and guns and soldiers.

- She needed more money to run the country.

Elizabeth and law

Sometimes Elizabeth needed to pass laws. There were laws about how to treat the poor, and laws about religion and so on.

Elizabeth and Parliament

Under Henry VIII, Parliament had got used to meeting more often. The Members of Parliament wanted a say in what laws were made and how the country was run. They knew Elizabeth needed money from them. So she had to listen.

Parliament wanted all sorts of new laws on religion. But Elizabeth said no. Parliament also wanted to tell the Queen who to marry. She told them to mind their own business. But the battle went on. If the Queen said no too often, Parliament would not give her any money.

Source C

Written by a modern historian.

Elizabeth only called Parliament thirteen times in the forty-four years of her reign.

For Elizabeth, Members of Parliament were little boys. They were a waste of an intelligent woman's time.

Source D

For everyday work, Elizabeth had advisers. They met several times a week. They worked on things like helping English merchants abroad, stopping new building in London and training soldiers.

The most important advisers in the middle of Elizabeth's reign were:

- **Lord Burghley**

- **Earl of Leicester**

- **Sir Francis Knollys**

- **Earl of Lincoln**

- **Sir Francis Walsingham**

- **Sir Christopher Hatton**

- **Sir James Croft.**

Running the country – Sir William Petre

Kings and queens needed people to run the country every day. This was Sir William Petre's job. He was born in 1506. He studied law and was a friend of Anne Boleyn's father. He got a job working on Henry VIII's divorce. He did other jobs for the King and became a Member of Parliament too.

Sir William Petre and Edward VI

After Henry died, Sir William worked for young King Edward. One of his jobs was to talk to Princess Mary. He had to try and get her to give up being a Catholic. He also checked on books that were published. No Catholic books were allowed.

Sir William Petre and Mary

Edward died and Sir William worked for Queen Mary. But he retired in 1553 because he was not very well. After that, he worked part time.

Sir William Petre and Elizabeth

Sir William worked for Queen Elizabeth for a little while. But he was not well. He wrote to a friend in 1565: *I have recovered from fever but am still a little deaf. I shall take medicine for the pain from my head to my shoulders.*

Sir William died in 1572. His wife was a Catholic. She built priestholes at the family home.

This was a very unusual thing for her to do. One of her husband's jobs had been to stop the Catholic religion from spreading.

Source E

Sir William Petre.

Questions

1 How often did Elizabeth call parliaments?

2 Why did Elizabeth tell the Members of Parliament to mind their own business?

3 When was Sir William Petre born?

4 How many kings and queens did Sir William Petre work for?

Very few people wrote about what Elizabeth I looked like.

Pictures of Elizabeth

There are quite a lot of pictures of Elizabeth. But kings and queens always wanted to look good. They did not pay painters to make them look weak and ugly.

Elizabeth made sure that paintings showed her looking good.

There was no television or newspapers then, and travel was difficult. So few people would ever see the Queen.

Source A

Elizabeth as a young girl in 1546.

Source B

Elizabeth in 1583.

Source C

Elizabeth in 1600.

Source D

Elizabeth in 1588.

Questions

1 Look at Sources A–E.

   a Write one sentence to describe what Elizabeth looks like in each of the pictures.

   b How old do you think she looks in each picture? (Just put **young** or **old**.)

2 Elizabeth was born in 1533 and died in 1603. Write down how old she was in each picture.

3 Which picture is:

   a most real looking

   b most unreal looking?

   Give one reason for each of your answers.

4 Read Source H.

   What two things tell you that Elizabeth is quite old by this time?

Source E

Elizabeth in about 1600, but painted after her death in 1603.

Source F

An order made in 1563.

No one will paint a picture of the Queen until a very good painter has painted her picture.

Then all other painters must paint the Queen in the same way.

Source G

A foreigner described Elizabeth in 1574.

She is tall and well formed with a good skin, though rather dark. She has fine eyes.

Source H

Another foreigner described Elizabeth in 1598.

Her face is good-looking but wrinkled. Her eyes are small, black and pleasant. Her nose is hooked, her lips narrow. She has a red wig.

Life in the country

Most people lived in villages in the country. They worked on the land in big, open fields. A few rich people did not have to work in the fields. They paid workers to farm for them.

A new way of farming – enclosure

The old way of farming was in big fields that everyone shared. The new way of farming was in small fields that were fenced in. These fields were not shared. This way of farming with small fields was called **enclosure**. More and more farmers wanted enclosure in Tudor times.

Hard work and leisure

The farm workers worked from dawn to nightfall. They ploughed. They sowed seed. They cut the wheat. They looked after the animals. But they did have some holidays (holy days). One holiday was May Day. There was dancing and drinking and football.

The size of towns

The biggest town in Tudor times was London, which had 100,000 people. The next biggest towns were Norwich, Bristol and York. But none of these had more than 20,000 people – the size of a small town today.

Houses in the towns

Houses in the towns were jammed close together. Sometimes people could touch each other across the street from their top windows.

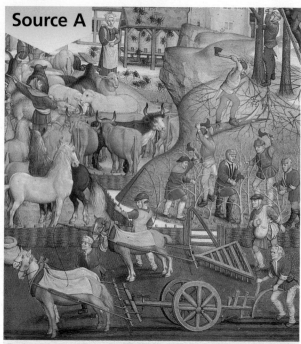

Source A

Work in a Tudor village.

Filthy towns

The towns were filthy. There were no flushing toilets. All rubbish and human waste went into the street or river. Many people died from diseases.

Markets

Big towns had markets. Farmers and their families came to towns and sold sheep, cows, eggs and milk in the market.

There were shops all round the market. There were shoe menders, barbers, dentists and lots of pubs. Market day was a good time to meet friends, have a drink and buy some things in the town.

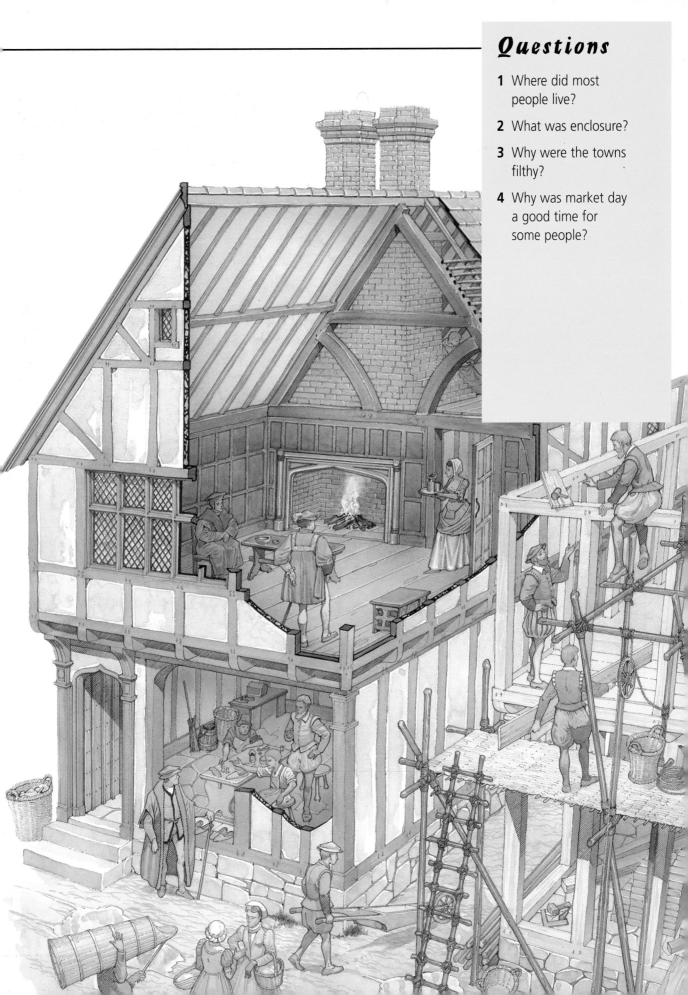

Questions

1 Where did most people live?

2 What was enclosure?

3 Why were the towns filthy?

4 Why was market day a good time for some people?

There were four sorts of doctors:

1 Physicians

Physicians were the top doctors. They were trained at university. They studied for many years. They charged a lot of money.

2 Barber surgeons

Barbers cut hair. So many people thought they must be good at cutting off arms and legs too. (There were no **anaesthetics** then.) Physicians looked down on barber surgeons. They thought they were like butchers.

3 Apothecaries

Apothecaries mixed up medicines for physicians. They also sold the medicines themselves. They did not charge as much as physicians.

4 Midwives

Women were not allowed to go to university. A woman was allowed to be a midwife. A midwife delivered babies.

Treating illness

The ways of treating illness were often very different from today.

However, some common sense things, like resting if you were ill, were the same.

Many people believed that a king or queen could cure diseases like **scrofula** by touch.

Medicine and the Greeks

Many physicians used Greek ideas in medicine. The Greeks said there were four **humours** in the body. The four humours were:

- yellow bile
- black bile
- blood
- phlegm.

If the four humours were out of balance, a person became ill. For instance, if a person had too much blood, a physician made a cut and took some out.

Source A

Medicine and the stars

Many people believed in **astrology**. They said the moon and stars affected illness.

Everyday medicine

We do not know about everyday medicine for ordinary people. No one wrote it down.

Many people were treated by mothers, grandmothers and local wise women. They had a knowledge of herbs passed down by word of mouth.

Source B

A Tudor cure for **tuberculosis**.

Take a nine day old pig. Add spearmint, turnip, celery, nine dates and cinnamon. Cook. Put the juice in a glass in the sun for nine days. Drink nine spoonfuls.

Source C

From the account book at Hengrave Hall in 1573.

Reward for letting my mistress' blood 2 shillings.

LADY GRACE MILDMAY

Growing up

Lady Grace Mildmay was born in 1552. She was brought up strictly.

Marrying

Lady Grace married Anthony Mildmay in 1567. He was not keen on the marriage. He spent a lot of time away from home.

Lady Grace's day

Lady Grace spent her time reading the Bible, playing the lute, sewing and looking after sick people.

Lady Grace and medicine

Lady Grace became very interested in medicine. She grew herbs and made medicines. She kept a notebook of the herbs she used. That is how we know about her work.

Lady Grace became very skilled. She treated everything from **smallpox** and skin disease to unwanted pregnancies.

Questions

1 a Write down the four sorts of doctors in Tudor times.
   b Write down what each one did.

2 Write three sentences about Lady Grace Mildmay.

3 How do we know about Lady Grace Mildmay's use of herbs?

4 Why do you think the mistress of Hengrave Hall (Source C) paid someone to 'let' her blood?

The number of poor people increased in Tudor times. There were three reasons for this:

1 There were a million more people by the year 1600. So there were more people looking for work, and there was not enough food.

2 Farmers kept more of their sheep in the new enclosures (small fields). One shepherd could look after a lot of sheep. So there were fewer jobs.

3 More people wanted to buy more things, so prices went up. Poor people were left behind.

Source A

These houses were built at Hengrave Hall for family servants and the deserving poor.

What rich people thought

Some rich people were afraid when they saw lots of poor people. They thought the poor people might try to attack them, or steal their things.

There were two types of poor people:

1 The deserving poor

Some people could not help being poor. They were too sick, too old or too young to work. People thought they should help them.

2 Sturdy beggars

These were people who were fit and well, but who did not want to work. Some of them wandered from village to village. They begged or worked a bit. Many people thought they should be punished.

Punishments

Because rich people were afraid of them, sturdy beggars were often punished severely. Some were **branded** on the ear. Others were whipped in the street. If they carried on begging, they might even be hanged.

What did the government do?

The government wanted to help the deserving poor. It passed some laws in Parliament:

1572 The rich must pay some money to help the deserving poor.

1597 Sturdy beggars found wandering must be whipped and sent back to their home village.

1601 Towns and villages must collect money to help the deserving poor.

Source B

A sturdy beggar being whipped.

Source C

This story comes from a book of 1567. We do not know if it is true.

Nicholas Jennings the beggar

Nicholas Jennings was begging in London. He was dressed in rags and covered in blood and dirt.

Found out by two boys

Two boys saw him smear the blood and dirt on himself. They fetched a constable. Nicholas had lots of money on him (twenty times as much money as a good worker could earn in a day).

Nicholas washed

When Nicholas was washed, they found he was fit and well.

Source D

From the account books of Hengrave Hall. Gifts to the poor.

To old John	12 pence
To the collector of the poor	12 pence
For a pair of shoes for a servant boy	13 pence

Questions

1 Write down the three reasons why the number of poor people increased in Tudor times.

2 a How many sorts of poor people were there?
b Who were the deserving poor?
c Who were sturdy beggars?

3 Look at all the sources. Which sources tell you some people were kind to the poor?

Explorers

Explorers are people who look for new lands. In Tudor times many men sailed from England and Europe to find new lands. Christopher Columbus was a famous explorer. He discovered the West Indies. You can see this in the map below.

Merchants

Exploring was exciting. But there was money to be made too. Merchants are people who buy and sell all sorts of things from fish to gold.

What merchants wanted

Merchants wanted to buy silk, jewels and spices from the East. They wanted to buy furs and wood from Russia. They could sell all these things in England.

Merchants and slaves

Sometimes they bought and sold people as **slaves**. They bought them in Africa and sold them in the West Indies.

Selling English wool

It was all very well buying things. But merchants had to sell things too. They sold English wool all over the world.

Where English wool went

Clothes made from English wool went as far away as China and India. Men like Thomas Kytson of Hengrave Hall made a lot of money from selling wool.

Source A

From the Johnson Letters. The Johnsons were Tudor merchants. These are some things they had bought to sell in England.

My master has asked me to write thanking you for the parcels.

12 lb pepper

1 lb cloves

1/2 lb mace

l lb grains

l lb nutmeg

2 lb ginger

1 green carpet

1 lb cinnamon

1 box fruit in sugar

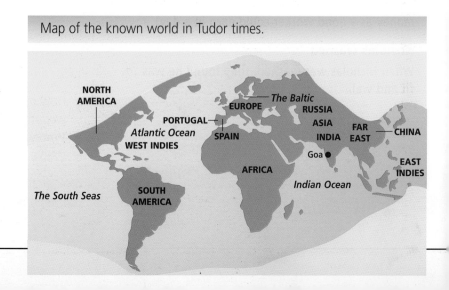
Map of the known world in Tudor times.

Wars

Many countries wanted to own new lands. Then their merchants could buy and sell things in these new lands.

This meant that countries like England and Spain went to war about who should own new lands.

Source B

Written by a Spanish spy in England in 1586.

Francis Drake has returned from the Indies. He captured several of our towns. He took 140 cannons, £1,000 of pearls, £70,000 of gold and silver.

Source C

A carving at Hengrave Hall. The figure of Death is wearing a woollen **shroud**. Queen Elizabeth ordered that everyone must be buried in woollen shrouds. This meant more wool was sold.

Questions

1 What is an explorer?

2 Find the names of two famous explorers on these pages.

3 What is a merchant?

4 What sort of things did Tudor merchants buy?

5 What did Tudor merchants sell all over the world?

SIR FRANCIS DRAKE

Sir Francis Drake was a great seaman and explorer. He attacked the Spanish in the West Indies (see map page 36).

He sailed round the world in 1577 in his ship the *Golden Hind*.

Elizabeth knighted him. (Made him Sir Francis Drake.)

He helped to defeat the Spanish Armada in 1588.

London people loved going to the **theatre**. At first actors put on plays in pubs and markets.

Theatres in London

Then James Burbage built a theatre in 1576. Soon there were several theatres. The Globe Theatre was a famous theatre.

There were also theatres called the Rose, the Swan and the Curtain. All the theatres were very much alike. They looked like the picture on this page. The centre part was open to the sky.

Putting on a play

The actors put up a flag if the weather was good enough for a play. People could see it from a long way away.

When a play was about to start, a trumpet was blown. Then, while the play was on a white flag flew over the theatre.

All the money for the tickets was kept in a box in a small office. We get the name 'box office' from this.

Watching a play

Poor people paid one penny. They stood in front of the stage. Richer people sat further back. Food and drink was on sale all the time. People laughed and talked. If they did not like the play they threw rotten eggs at the actors.

There were always a lot of pickpockets about. This made many people think that theatres were dangerous and wicked places.

Writers

William Shakespeare (1564–1616) is still the most famous writer of plays in the world. He wrote 38 plays. These include *Romeo and Juliet.* Christopher Marlowe was another famous writer.

Actors

There were usually about twelve actors in a play.

All the actors were male. Boys played the part of women. Most groups of actors had a patron. The patron was an important rich person. He helped the group of actors by giving them money.

Source A

This was written by a Puritan in 1518.

One trumpet blow brings 1,000 people to watch a play. While a church bell only brings 100 to church.

Source B

From a diary in the 1590s.

If more than 30 people a week die of the plague in London all the theatres will be closed.

Source C

London people walked across London Bridge to watch a play at the Globe Theatre. It was about a ten minute walk.

Questions

1 Where did actors put plays on at first?

2 What did William Shakespeare and Christopher Marlowe do?

3 Read Source B.

Why do you think the theatres were closed if there were a lot of people dying of the plague?

3.6 CHRISTOPHER MARLOWE: A MURDER MYSTERY?

It was 30 May 1593. Four men, including Christopher Marlowe, met at a house near London. They spent the day talking. No one knows what it was about.

Then, in the evening, a row broke out. Marlowe hit one of the others on the head with the handle of a dagger. They fought. Somehow the dagger stabbed Marlowe in the right eye. He died instantly.

Who were the four men?

All four men were probably government spies. They did jobs such as spying on English Catholics in France and in England.

One of the four men worked for Thomas Walsingham, who helped his cousin run the secret spy service for Queen Elizabeth. Christopher Marlowe himself worked as a spy.

Was Marlowe's death an accident or murder?

The man who stabbed Marlowe was let off. It was called self-defence. But only the four men in the room knew what really happened.

Marlowe was an atheist. An atheist is someone who says there is no God. This was very serious in Tudor England.

If Marlowe was found guilty of being an atheist, he would have been tortured and then killed.

What might Marlowe have said under torture? He might have given away names of other atheists. Maybe someone wanted to make sure Marlowe never lived to do this.

This may be a picture of Marlowe when he was twenty-one years old.

Source A

Source B

From a modern history book, 1992.

Marlowe is remembered as a writer, an atheist, a homosexual and a man who lived fast and died young.

Marlowe's last days

18 May

Privy Council

Marlowe was accused of writing that there was no God.

18–30 May

Marlowe was allowed to go free. He had to report to the Privy Council every day.

30 May

The Privy Council got a report that Marlowe was an atheist and had important friends. If this was believed, Marlowe would be tortured and killed. He might give away the names of his important friends. **Who were they?**

30 May 6 p.m.

Marlowe was stabbed to death.

Source C

Francis Walsingham, who ran Queen Elizabeth's secret spy service.

Source D

This is from a report to the government about Christopher Marlowe.

Marlowe said that Christ was illegitimate, that Christ deserved to die and that, if there is a God or religion, it is the Catholics'.

Questions

1 What is an atheist?

2 How did Marlowe die?

3 Can you suggest any ideas about why he died?

Religion was very important to people during Tudor and Stuart times. Everyone believed in God and Jesus Christ.

Roman Catholics

Up to the reign of Henry VIII (1509–1547) everyone was a Roman Catholic. Henry broke away from the Catholic Church. He started the Church of England (or **Anglican Church**). Most people in England were now Protestants. The few Catholics left were forced to worship in secret.

Protestants

The Protestants in the Church of England split into two groups. Each group had its own idea about how to worship God.

- The Laudians wanted bishops and colourful churches.

- The Puritans wanted simple, plain churches and no bishops.

In the 1600s some Protestants left the Church of England. They included the Quakers and the Baptists. These groups were called **Dissenters** because they went against the Church of England.

Religious groups in the seventeenth century.

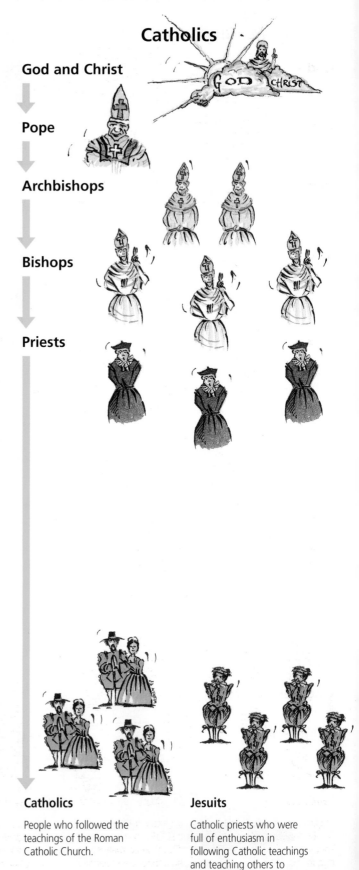

Catholics

God and Christ

Pope

Archbishops

Bishops

Priests

Catholics

People who followed the teachings of the Roman Catholic Church.

Jesuits

Catholic priests who were full of enthusiasm in following Catholic teachings and teaching others to do so.

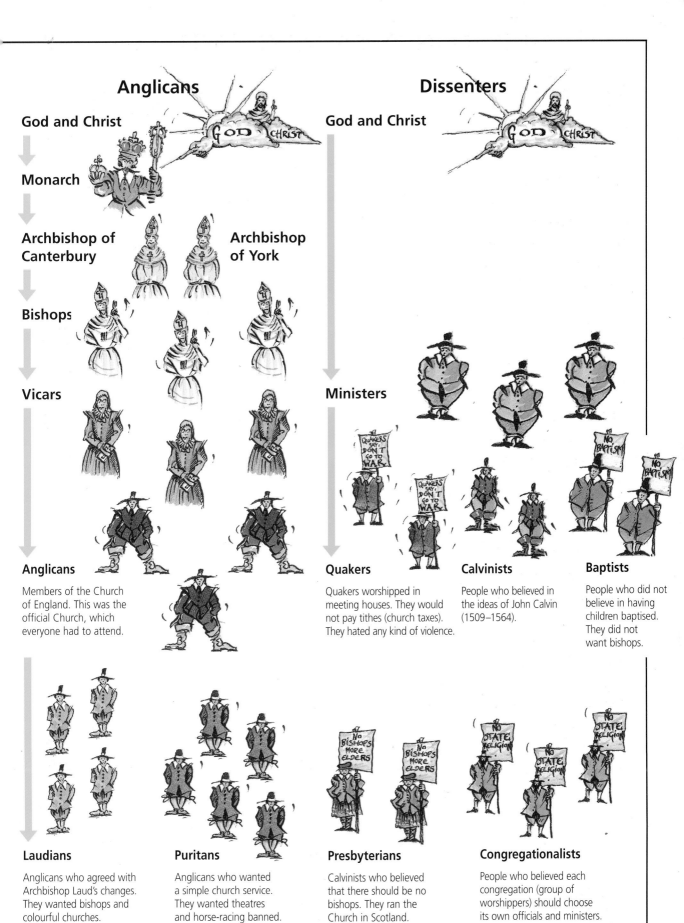

Anglicans

God and Christ

Monarch

Archbishop of Canterbury   **Archbishop of York**

Bishops

Vicars

Anglicans

Members of the Church of England. This was the official Church, which everyone had to attend.

Dissenters

God and Christ

Ministers

Quakers

Quakers worshipped in meeting houses. They would not pay tithes (church taxes). They hated any kind of violence.

Calvinists

People who believed in the ideas of John Calvin (1509–1564).

Baptists

People who did not believe in having children baptised. They did not want bishops.

Laudians

Anglicans who agreed with Archbishop Laud's changes. They wanted bishops and colourful churches.

Puritans

Anglicans who wanted a simple church service. They wanted theatres and horse-racing banned.

Presbyterians

Calvinists who believed that there should be no bishops. They ran the Church in Scotland.

Congregationalists

People who believed each congregation (group of worshippers) should choose its own officials and ministers.

A new king

Elizabeth I died in 1603. James I became the King of England.

High hopes

Both the Catholics and the Puritans hoped that James would be on their side. Both groups were left disappointed.

James I and Church matters

1 James I and the Catholics

James I was a Protestant. He did nothing to help the Catholics. He told Catholic priests to leave England. This made the Catholics angry.

2 James I meets the Puritans

In 1604 James I met the Puritans at Hampton Court. The Puritans said they did not want to have any bishops. But James did not agree. He sent the Puritans away. This made the Puritans angry.

3 A new Bible

In 1611 James I published a new Bible. It was written in English, not Latin. Now everyone could understand the Bible better.

Charles I

James I died in 1625. His son became king – Charles I.

Source A

James next to his mother Mary, Queen of Scots. It shows the year as 1583. But James never saw his mother again after 1567. The artist has made the picture up!

Source B

James I said this in 1604.

The Puritans must do as they are told, or I will chase them out of the country.

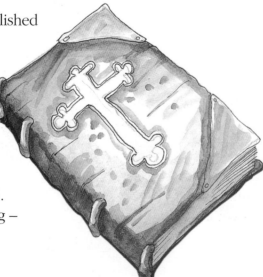

Source C

A cartoon drawn in 1637. It shows Laud with three Puritans who have had their ears cut off. One of the Puritans, William Prynne, is holding his head where his ears were. The ears are on a plate in front of Laud.

Source D

James I said this to Parliament in 1609.

Charles I agreed with what he said.

Kings are sent by God to rule over people.

No person on earth has more power than the King.

Parliament cannot tell the King what to do. Only God has more power than the King.

Charles I and Church matters

1 Archbishop Laud

In 1633 Charles I made William Laud the Archbishop of Canterbury. Charles and Laud made some changes to the Church of England. They said churches should have stained-glass windows and colourful paintings on the walls.

2 Laud and the Puritans

Puritans did not want these changes. So Laud banned Puritan books and had some Puritans put into prison. Others had their ears cut off (see Source C).

3 Puritans leave England

Some Puritans went to America. There they could worship in the way they wanted (see pages 48 and 49).

Trouble ahead!

Parliament did not like the changes that Laud and Charles I made to the Church. In the end, Charles and Parliament went to war.

Questions

1 Read page 44.

Copy the sentences below. Choose one of the words in italics.

James I made both the Catholics and the Puritans *happy/angry/delighted*. In 1611 James I published a new Bible. It was written in *Latin/English*.

2 Read **Charles I and Church matters**.

   a What changes did Charles I and Laud make to the Church of England?
   b Why did this anger the Puritans?
   c What did Laud do to the Puritans?
   d What did some Puritans do after this?

3 Read Source D.

   Did James I and Charles I believe that kings had more power or less power than Parliament?

Source A

my lord out of the loue i beare ~~vnto~~ To some of youere freuds i haue a caer of youer preseruacion therfor i woufd... aduyse yowe as yolhe Teuder youer Lyf To deuys some epscuse To shift of youer aHendance at This parleament

Part of the letter sent to Lord Monteagle on 4 November 1605.

It is telling him not to go to the Houses of Parliament.

Angry Catholics

Catholics were angry that James I had done nothing to help them. Catholics wanted to worship in their own way, but James I would not let them.

The plot

Some Catholics were so angry that they made up a plot.

James I had to open Parliament on 5 November 1605. The plot was to blow up the Houses of Parliament and kill James.

Gunpowder

The plotters rented a cellar underneath the Houses of Parliament. They hid thirty-six barrels of gunpowder in the cellar.

A letter

On 4 November, a Catholic called Lord Monteagle received a letter. It told him not to go to Parliament the next day.

Guy Fawkes

Lord Monteagle gave the letter to the government. Soldiers were sent to search the cellar.

The soldiers found Guy Fawkes and the gunpowder. Fawkes was tortured and owned up. The plotters were later executed.

Bonfires

People were angry when they heard about the plot. Now Catholics were hated more than ever. Protestants lit bonfires to show they were glad that the plot had failed.

Guy Fawkes' signature before and after he was tortured.

Source B

SUPPLICIUM
De octo coniuratis sumtum in Britannia,
diebus 30. et 31. Jan. Styl. vet. Anno CIƆ. IƆCVII.
sumtum quidem separatim de quaternis,
Sed tamen propter eandem omnino Supplicii
rationem, hac tabella coniunctim expressum.

Iustitia   *Fama*

Some of the gunpowder plotters.

Thomas Percy   *Guy Fawkes*   *Robert Catesby*

A print showing the execution of the gunpowder plotters.

Questions

1 Read **Angry Catholics**.

Why were Catholics angry with James I?

2 Read **The plot** and **Gunpowder.**

What did some Catholics plan to do?

3 Read **A letter** and **Guy Fawkes**.

   a What did the letter to Lord Monteagle say?

   b What did he do?

   c What did the soldiers do?

   d What happened to Guy Fawkes?

Unhappy Puritans

Many Puritans were unhappy with James I. He would not let them worship in the way they wanted to.

A new country – a new life

One group of Puritans decided to go to America. Here they could worship as they wanted. They would live simple lives. James I would not be able to bother them.

The journey

On 16 September 1620, a ship called the *Mayflower* set sail for America. There were 100 Puritans on board. They became known as the **Pilgrim Fathers**. Pilgrims are people who go on religious journeys.

The journey was terrible. The ship was too crowded. They soon ran out of fresh food.

There were lots of storms. Many of the Pilgrims were seasick. Some fell ill with diarrhoea.

On 20 December 1620, the *Mayflower* finally arrived in America.

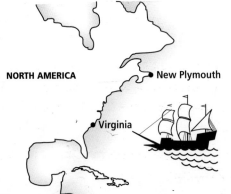

NORTH AMERICA

New Plymouth

Virginia

Source A

From a modern history book.

The Pilgrims called their town New Plymouth. They built a big wooden church there. Now they could worship God in peace.

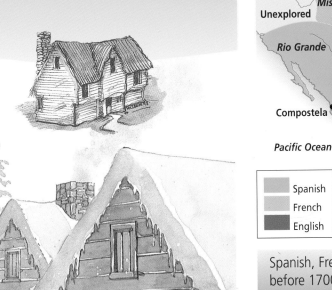

Spanish, French and English land in America before 1700.

Questions

1 Read **A new country – a new life**.

   Why did the Puritans go to America?

2 Read **Starting a new life**.

   Why were things hard to begin with?

3 Read **Help arrives**.

   How did the Indians help the Pilgrims to survive?

Starting a new life

Where the Pilgrims landed was cold and empty. They had to start a town from scratch. They built log houses to live in.

Life was hard to begin with. The Pilgrims planted seeds, but they did not grow. In the first year, half the Pilgrims died from illness or hunger. It looked as if they would all die.

Help arrives

Then some Indians showed them how to make the crops grow well. They planted corn, pumpkins and beans. The harvest of 1621 was very good. There was plenty of food.

The Pilgrims celebrated with the Indians. They feasted on roast turkey and goose, and they gave thanks to God for the harvest.

Soon they were joined by other Puritans from England.

James VI of Scotland

James Stuart was born in 1566. He became King James VI of Scotland when he was just one year old!

James was an unhappy child. He was lonely and his teachers bullied him.

But James was very clever. He read lots of books and knew a lot of things. When he grew up, he turned out to be one of Scotland's best kings.

James I of England

Just before she died in 1603, Elizabeth I said she wanted James to become king.

James was very pleased to be the new King of England.

Most English people were pleased too. James was a Protestant and this was what they wanted.

As James travelled to London, people lined the way. They cheered and wished him luck.

Would James I be a good king?

Source A

James I of England.

Source B

Written by an Englishman in 1650.

James was fat. His eyes were large and rolling. His tongue was too large for his mouth. His drink used to dribble from his mouth. He never washed his hands. James was clever about small things, but a fool about things that mattered.

James I and Parliament

James believed that he was the most powerful person in the country. Only God had more power than him. He soon fell out with Parliament. Why was this?

1 James had money problems

James liked spending money. Parliament thought he spent too much and it would not let him raise taxes. James started to borrow money from banks. Parliament did not like this.

2 James had favourites

James chose his own ministers (people who helped him rule). His **favourite** minister was George Villiers, the Duke of Buckingham. James paid him lots of money and gave him presents. Parliament did not like this.

3 James told Parliament off

Parliament did not like the way James ran the country. James told Parliament to mind its own business. He said Parliament could not tell him how to run the country.

James was mistaken

Falling out with Parliament was a mistake. James should have realised that he needed Parliament's help to run the country well.

The wisest fool?

James I is often nicknamed the 'wisest fool in **Christendom**' (the part of the world where Christians lived). This is because he was clever, but he still made mistakes in running the country.

Source C

Written by a modern historian.

James I was clever. But he was soft with people. One minute he was telling them off, the next he gave in to them. He took too much notice of his favourites and could be big-headed.

Source D

James I said this in 1621.

Parliament has too much to say. I am surprised English kings have allowed this.

Questions

1 Make a bigger copy of this diagram.

Good   Bad

2 Read Source B and Source C.

   a Put James I's **good points** on your diagram.

   b Put James I's **bad points** on your diagram.

3 Read **James I and Parliament**.

   Write down three reasons why James fell out with Parliament.

4 Do you agree that James was 'the wisest fool in Christendom'? Explain your answer.

Charles I quarrels with Parliament

When James I died in 1625, his son Charles became king. Charles I soon fell out with Parliament. Why was this?

1 Money

Charles I spent a lot of money on his friends and on fighting wars against France and Spain. He kept asking Parliament for more money. But Parliament said he should cut down his spending.

2 Power

Charles believed he had the power to run the country without Parliament. He did not like Parliament telling him what to do.

Charles decides to rule on his own

Charles grew tired of Parliament's complaints. In 1629 he decided to rule by himself. Parliament did not meet again until 1640.

Ship Money

Charles needed to raise some money. Ship Money was an old tax that sea ports paid during wartime. The money was used to pay for the navy.

In 1635 there was no war on. But Charles said the whole country had to pay Ship Money. This made many people angry.

Source A

A **civil war** is when two sides from the same country fight each other.

King

V

Parliament

The English Civil War was between the King and Parliament.

Source B

The *Sovereign of the Seas*, built in 1637. It was paid for out of Ship Money.

John Hampden

John Hampden said that Ship Money was against the law and he would not pay it. Hampden was taken to court. The judges ordered him to pay, even though half of them agreed with him!

Charles I was becoming very unpopular.

Church matters again

Many Members of Parliament were Puritans. Charles brought back stained-glass windows in churches. He also allowed priests to wear colourful robes. The Puritans did not like this.

Charles angers the Scots

In 1637 Charles made a big mistake. He told the Scots to use the English Prayer Book in their churches. The Scots were furious.

Riots broke out during church services in Scotland. A Scottish army marched into England.

Without Parliament to vote him taxes, Charles had no money. He could not afford to raise an army to fight the Scots.

Charles was forced to call Parliament to ask for some money.

May 1640: Parliament meets

When Parliament met, it was in an angry mood. The Members of Parliament had not met for eleven years. They had lots of complaints about Charles.

The Members of Parliament said they would not give Charles any money, unless he listened to their complaints. But Charles would not listen. He ended Parliament after three weeks.

Source C

The Arch-Prelate of St Andrewes in Scotland reading the new Service-booke in his pontificall assaulted by men & women, with Cricketts stooles Stickes and Stones

A cartoon from 1637. It shows a riot in a Scottish church.

Questions

1 Read Source A. What is a civil war?

2 Read **Charles I quarrels with Parliament**.

 What two things did Charles I and Parliament argue about?

3 Read **Charles angers the Scots**.

 What made the Scots riot?

4 Read **May 1640: Parliament meets**.

 Why did Parliament meet?

The Scots again

The Scots said they would go back to Scotland if Charles gave them some money. Charles agreed, even though he still did not have any money! He was forced to call Parliament again.

November 1640: Parliament meets again

The Members of Parliament were led by John Pym. They were still angry with Charles. Before they would give Charles any money, they made him agree to their demands.

Charles gives in

Charles agreed to:

- call Parliament every three years

- not tax people without asking Parliament first

- stop the changes made to the Church by William Laud.

Parliament now gave Charles money to pay off the Scots.

Laud and Strafford

The hated Laud was put in prison. Parliament said Thomas Strafford should be executed. (Strafford had helped Charles to run the country between 1629 and 1640.) Charles agreed to this.

Rebellion in Ireland

In 1641 Catholics in Ireland rebelled. Charles asked Parliament for money to raise an army against the Irish. But Parliament would not agree. It did not want Charles to be in charge of an army. He might use it to fight against Parliament.

A scene from the film *Cromwell*. Charles is looking for the five MPs.

Questions

1 Read **Civil War breaks out** on page 55.

   Why was the war fought?

2 Look at the diagram at the bottom of page 55.

   a What nickname was given to the King's side?

   b What nickname was given to Parliament's?

Charles loses his temper

Charles was especially fed up with John Pym and four other Members of Parliament. He decided to go to the Houses of Parliament and arrest them.

On 4 January 1642 Charles burst into Parliament with some soldiers. But the MPs had been warned. They were not there. Charles was angry and called out: *I see the birds are flown!*

Charles had been made to look very silly. Things between Parliament and Charles were very bad. They hated each other. Only a war would settle their quarrel.

Civil war breaks out

In August 1642 Charles raised his flag at Nottingham. This showed that he was at war with Parliament. Charles got an army together, and Parliament raised its own army to fight him.

The Civil War had begun. It was fought to see who should run the country: the King or Parliament.

The two sides

For the King – the Cavaliers	For Parliament – the Roundheads
Lords	MPs
Landowners	Merchants
Anglicans	Puritans

Families split

Many families were split over which side to be on. Fathers fought sons, and brothers fought brothers.

Weapons

Most of the fighting in the Civil War was hand to hand. The main weapons were:

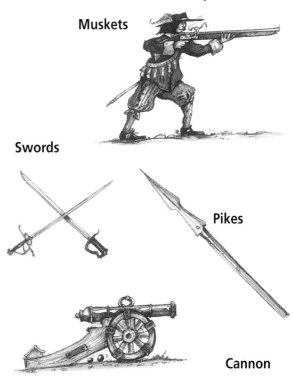

Muskets

Swords

Pikes

Cannon

Source E

From a modern history book.

The north and west of England supported King Charles I.

The south and east of England, including London, supported Parliament.

Charles beaten

The Civil War lasted until 1646. Charles I lost the war. He gave himself up to the Scots. The Scots handed him over to Parliament.

Why did Parliament win the Civil War?

There were four reasons why Parliament won:

1 Parliament had better generals

The Royalists' best general was Prince Rupert. He was very brave and dashing. His cavalry charged the enemy at top speed. But he sometimes acted rashly and also lost control of his men.

Parliament's best general was Oliver Cromwell. He made few mistakes and his soldiers always carried out orders.

Cromwell

Prince Rupert

Question

List four reasons why Parliament won the Civil War.

The main battles of the English Civil War.

Royalists   **Parliamentarians**

Edgehill
October 1642 — Draw

Newbury
September 1643 — Draw

Marston Moor
July 1644 — Victory for Parliament and Scots

Naseby
June 1645 — Victory for Parliament

Preston
August 1648 — Parliament smashes Royalists and Scots

2 Other kings did not help Charles

Charles hoped kings from other countries would help him to fight Parliament. But no other king joined him.

In 1644 the Scots sent 20,000 men to fight on Parliament's side. The Scots helped Parliament to win the Battle of Marston Moor.

3 Parliament had the New Model Army

In 1644 Oliver Cromwell and Sir Thomas Fairfax formed the New Model Army to fight for Parliament. The soldiers in it were:

- well trained
- disciplined
- well paid
- well equipped
- well fed.

The Royalists laughed at it and called it the *New Noddle Army*!

But they were wrong to laugh. The New Model Army was very strong. It beat the King's army at Naseby in 1645.

4 Charles ran out of money

Charles lost a lot of men at Naseby.

He did not have enough money to raise another army.

Parliament was given money by rich merchants.

Parliament was also better at collecting taxes than the King.

A modern painting of a Royalist charge at the Battle of Edgehill in 1642.

Source A

Parliament talks to Charles

In 1646 Parliament started to talk to Charles about the way England would be run. Parliament did not want to kill Charles.

The army takes a hand

Now the war was over, Parliament told the army to go home. But the soldiers would not go because their wages had not been paid.

Instead the army took Charles prisoner. Now the army started to talk to Charles about peace.

Charles cannot be trusted

The army thought the talks were going well. Then Charles escaped to the Isle of Wight (a small island off the south coast of England). From there he made a deal with the Scots.

The Scots agreed to fight for Charles. The army was furious. Charles had shown that he could not be trusted.

The Battle of Preston, 1648

At this battle, the Scots were beaten by Cromwell's New Model Army.

The army said that Charles was a traitor and should die.

What about Parliament?

Some Members of Parliament thought Charles should live. The army went to the Houses of Parliament and threw out those who were on Charles' side.

The MPs who were left were called the **Rump**.

Charles put on trial

The Rump of MPs said Charles should be put on trial.

At the trial, Charles would not take his hat off because he did not want to show respect. He said that the court did not have the power to put the King on trial.

The court said Charles was a traitor and a murderer.

Source A

The hat worn by John Bradshaw, the chief judge at Charles' trial. It was strengthened inside by metal.

Source B

Over fifty judges signed Charles' death warrant. One of them was Oliver Cromwell. This is his signature.

Source C

The execution of Charles I in 1649.

Charles found guilty

Charles was found guilty by the court. John Bradshaw put on a red gown and told Charles that his head was to be chopped off.

Charles goes to his death

Charles was executed on 30 January 1649. It was very cold. He wore two shirts. He did not want the crowd to think he was shivering from fear.

Charles put his head on the block. His head was chopped off with one blow of the axe. People in the crowd were shocked by what they saw.

Questions

1 Read page 58. Write out these events in the order in which they happened:

- The Rump of MPs said Charles should be put on trial.
- Charles escaped from the army.
- Charles made a deal with the Scots.
- Charles was taken prisoner by the army.
- The army beat the Scots at the Battle of Preston.

2 Read **Charles put on trial**.

   a What did the court say Charles had done?
   b What did Charles say to the court?

3 Read **Charles found guilty**.

   What did John Bradshaw do?

4 Look at Source A. Why do you think John Bradshaw's hat was strengthened with metal?

5 Read **Charles goes to his death**.

   Why did Charles wear two shirts?

5.5 OLIVER CROMWELL: PROTECTOR OR DICTATOR?

England now a republic

England no longer had a king. It was now a **republic**. A republic is a country that does not have a king or queen.

Cromwell falls out with Parliament

Oliver Cromwell was now the most powerful person in the country. He was supported by the army.

Cromwell soon fell out with the Rump Parliament. In 1653 he went to the Houses of Parliament with some soldiers. All the Rump MPs were thrown out (see Sources A and B).

The Barebones Parliament

Cromwell and the army chose 140 new Members of Parliament. They were all Puritans.

They were called the **Barebones Parliament** after one of the MPs – Praise-God Barebones.

The MPs were not very good. They quarrelled with each other. Soon they said that they did not want to do the job any more.

Cromwell becomes Lord Protector

In 1653 the army made Cromwell the **Lord Protector** (ruler) of England.

Cromwell was not liked. He put up taxes.

Some people were worried that Cromwell and the army had too much power. Cromwell took action to stop these people grumbling.

Source A

Cromwell said this when he threw out the Rump MPs in 1653.

Go, I say. Let's have done with you. In the name of God, go!

Cromwell throws out the Rump MPs. Drawn by a Dutch artist.

Source B

THIS HOVSE IS TO LET

Be gone you rogues
You have Sate long enough

60

The rule of the major-generals, 1655–1657

Cromwell put eleven army major-generals in charge. They were all strict Puritans. They stopped people enjoying themselves.

No theatres

No horse-racing

No festivities at Christmas

No bear-baiting

No drinking on Sundays

No swearing

The major-generals were very strict.

People hated the major-generals. Cromwell had to sack them in 1657.

Cromwell for king?

A lot of people thought England should have a king again. They asked Cromwell to be king, but he refused. He did not believe in kings. He had just fought a war to get rid of one!

Cromwell dies

Cromwell died in 1658. His son, Richard, became Lord Protector. He was so bad that he got the nickname 'Tumble-Down Dick'. Richard gave up after a year.

Source C

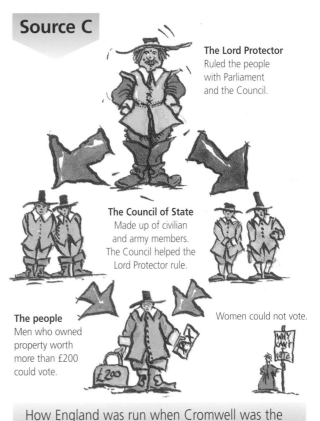

The Lord Protector
Ruled the people with Parliament and the Council.

The Council of State
Made up of civilian and army members. The Council helped the Lord Protector rule.

The people
Men who owned property worth more than £200 could vote.

Women could not vote.

How England was run when Cromwell was the Lord Protector.

Questions

1 Find Cromwell in Source B. What is he doing?

2 Read page 60. Copy these sentences. Fill in the gaps. Use the words in the box.

In _____ Cromwell became the _____ _____ of England.

The _____ ruled between 1655 and _____.

major-generals	Lord Protector
1657	1653

3 Read **The rule of the major-generals**.

Why were the major-generals hated?

The Civil War changed life in England. Many people said that the 'world had been turned upside down'.

The King had been executed and replaced by Cromwell, who was called the Lord Protector.

Ordinary people came up with ideas for running the country. They wrote leaflets and handed them out in the streets.

Who were these people and what ideas did they have?

Source A

> THE
> World turn'd upfide down:
> OR,
> A briefe defcription of the ridiculous Fashions of thefe diftracted Times.
> By T. J. a well-willer to King, Parliament and Kingdom.
>
> London: Printed for John Smith. 1646. 1 6 4 7. Jan: 26.

The front cover of a leaflet called *The World Turned Upside Down*, printed in about 1647.

The Fifth Monarchists

This group believed that Jesus was about to come back to earth. He would then rule the earth as the 'fifth monarch'.

The Diggers

The Diggers were led by Gerrard Winstanley. They said everyone was equal. Everyone had an equal right to share and farm the land.

IT'S ALL SO SIMPLE—JUST DIG AND SOW!

TWEET!!

COME AND DIG

NOT PRIVATE LAND

ALL MEN EQUAL HERE

YOU'RE DAMNED

The Muggletonians

This group believed that God had given them the power to say who should go to Heaven and who should go to Hell. They were led by John Reeve and Ludowicke Muggleton.

The Levellers

The Levellers were led by John Lilburne. They wanted England to be run by Parliament, not a king. Most men would be able to vote for MPs, not just the rich. A lot of men in the army were Levellers.

The Quakers

The Quakers were started by George Fox in 1652. They believed that everyone was equal. They would not pay tithes (taxes) to the Church of England.

The Ranters

The Ranters believed they were God's chosen people. They said they could do nothing wrong.

Questions

Look at the drawings.

1 a Who was the leader of the Levellers?
   b What did the Levellers want?

2 a Who was the leader of the Diggers?
   b What did the Diggers say?

Who were the Levellers?

The Levellers were a group of soldiers in the New Model Army. This army was led by Cromwell. It fought on the side of Parliament in the Civil War.

The Levellers said Parliament should speak for everyone, not just the rich.

The Levellers fall out with Cromwell

The Levellers did not like Cromwell.

- They said he was only bothered about rich farmers.

- They were angry that the army's wages had not been paid.

- In 1649 some Levellers found out that Cromwell was sending them to fight in Ireland. They thought he was doing this to get them out of the way.

The march to Burford

The Levellers said that they would not let Cromwell treat them like this.

They mutinied and refused to go to Ireland.

They left the army and went on a march, picking up supporters on the way.

On 13 May 1649, they reached Burford in Oxfordshire.

Source A

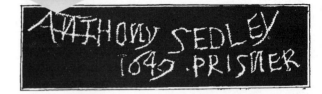

This name was carved into the font in Burford church. Anthony Sedley was one of the Levellers trapped in the church by Cromwell.

Source B

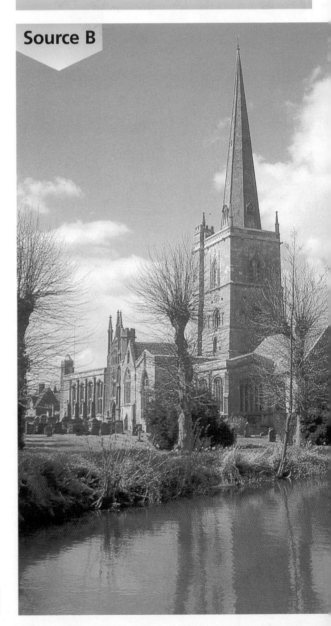

Burford church and churchyard.

Source C

From the Churchwardens' Account Book for Burford, 1649.

To Daniel Munke for cleaning the church when the Levellers were taken – 3s 6d [17.5p].

Cromwell attacks!

The Levellers set up camp for the night. But then they were attacked by a force led by Cromwell himself.

For three days, 340 Levellers were locked in Burford church. One of the Levellers carved his name on the font (see Source A).

The ringleaders executed

In the end, Cromwell had three of the ringleaders shot dead. The other Levellers were made to watch from the church roof.

Cromwell did not like the Levellers' ideas. By shooting the leaders, he was warning other people against following the Levellers.

Source D

From a leaflet written by the Levellers in 1649.

Cornet Den made an apology to Cromwell.

He said we were wrong and Cromwell was right.

Den howled and wept like a crocodile. He is a rogue and a villain.

The aims of the Levellers

The Levellers printed their aims in a leaflet in 1647.

- Parliament should meet every two years.

- Parliament should speak for everyone – not just the rich.

- All men should be allowed to vote (except servants and beggars).

- No more tithes (taxes) to the Church.

- People should be able to worship as they please.

Cornet Den

A fourth leader, called Cornet Den, should have been shot. But he begged Cromwell to forgive him.

Cromwell let him off.

The other Levellers were angry with Cornet Den. They said he was a rogue and a villain (see Source D).

Questions

1 Read page 64.

   a Who were the Levellers?
   b Why did the Levellers leave the army?

2 Read page 65. Why were the leaders shot?

Elizabeth's early life

Elizabeth Dysart was the daughter of William and Catherine Murray. Elizabeth was born in 1626.

The Murray family lived at Ham House in Surrey.

The Civil War

Charles I and William Murray were boyhood friends. Charles gave William a job in his government. William was on Charles' side in the Civil War.

William worked as a messenger for Charles. He carried letters to Charles' wife, who was living abroad. Charles made William the Count of Dysart as a reward.

After Charles I was executed in 1649, William fled to Holland.

Source A

Elizabeth Dysart as a young woman. She was known for her red hair.

Ham House. It was built in 1610 and is now owned by the National Trust.

Source B

Bishop Burnet said this about Elizabeth Dysart.

She was a clever woman, good at maths and history.

She was lively and chatty.

She was also friendly, but you would not want her for an enemy!

Friends with Cromwell

In 1648 Elizabeth married Sir Lionel Tollemache.

In the 1650s she became friendly with Oliver Cromwell, the Lord Protector of England. He visited Elizabeth's house. He liked her because she was witty and clever.

The Sealed Knot

Charles I's son, Charles Stuart, was living abroad in the 1650s. He wanted to return to England to be king. He had a lot of supporters in England.

The Sealed Knot was a secret society that smuggled letters to Charles. Elizabeth Dysart was in the Sealed Knot and carried its letters to Charles. It was dangerous work.

Source C

Elizabeth Dysart said this in 1658, when she heard that Cromwell had died.

All I can say is that I did know the 'old one'.

Source D

This was said of Elizabeth Dysart in 1677.

I went to see her at Ham House. She was very chatty. She was very beautiful when she was younger.

Was Elizabeth a double agent?

A double agent is someone who works for both sides at the same time. Some say Elizabeth was a double agent, working for both Cromwell and Charles Stuart.

Many historians say this is untrue:

1 Elizabeth and her family were strong supporters of the royal family. She probably would not have betrayed Charles Stuart.

2 Elizabeth's family was badly treated by Cromwell and Parliament in the Civil War. Parliament charged them heavy taxes and tried to take Ham House away from them.

Historians think Elizabeth made friends with Cromwell to cover up her membership of the Sealed Knot.

Charles II rewards Elizabeth

Charles Stuart returned to England in 1660. He became Charles II. He gave Elizabeth a pension of £800 as a reward for her help.

Questions

Read **Was Elizabeth a double agent?**

1 What is a double agent?

2 Do you think Elizabeth was a double agent? Give reasons for your answer.

5.9 FROM PROTECTOR TO THE ACT OF SETTLEMENT

England has a king again

Most people wanted to be ruled by a king again.

In 1660 Parliament asked Charles Stuart to come back to England as Charles II.

He arrived in England in May 1660. Crowds turned out to cheer him. They were pleased to have a king again.

It was called the **Restoration**.

A person who watched Charles II enter London wrote:

The roads were full of flowers. Bells were ringing.

There were trumpets and music.

There were so many people in the streets that it took seven hours to pass through the city.

Source A

Charles II, painted during his reign.

The merry monarch

Charles II was nicknamed 'The merry monarch'. This was because he liked having a good time.

He liked dancing, drinking wine and horse-racing. He was full of fun.

People were glad that the harsh rule of Cromwell was over.

Source B

Titus Oates in the pillory.

What was restored?

Charles II shows some mercy

Charles II did not want any more arguments. Most people who had fought against Charles I in the Civil War were pardoned.

Cromwell's body

Parliament said that Cromwell's body should be dug up. The body was hanged. Then his head was stuck on a pole for everyone to see.

The Church of England

Parliament said the Church of England was once again the official religion. It was against the law to worship in other churches.

Laws against Catholics and Puritans

Parliament passed laws against Catholics and Puritans. They were not allowed to be Members of Parliament, councillors or teachers.

The Popish Plot, 1678

In 1678 Titus Oates told the government that Catholics were plotting to kill Charles II. He said they were going to make England Catholic again.

People panicked. Innocent Catholics were beaten up in the streets. Some Catholics were killed.

In the end, it was found that Oates had been lying. In 1685 he was sentenced to life imprisonment and to be flogged in public once a year. But he was let out of prison in 1689.

Source C

A description of Titus Oates being flogged in 1686.

Oates was flogged so hard that the crowd took pity on him.

They called out, 'Enough, enough! Be easy on him.'

Questions

1 Read **England has a king again**.

   a When did Charles II come back to England?

   b What was it like in London when Charles II arrived?

2 Read **The merry monarch**.

   Why was Charles II called 'the merry monarch'?

3 Read **What was restored?**

   What happened to Cromwell's body?

The death of Charles II

Charles II died in 1685. He was replaced by his brother, James II.

The Duke of Monmouth's rebellion, 1685

James II was a Catholic. He was hard working and a brave soldier. Many thought he would be a good king. Despite his religion, people thought he should be given a chance.

The Duke of Monmouth was the nephew of James II. Monmouth did not trust James II. Monmouth said he was the rightful king.

Monmouth led an army of rebels against James II. But they were not very well armed. They were badly beaten by James at the Battle of Sedgemoor in 1685.

Judge Jeffreys

The rebels were captured and put on trial. Judge Jeffreys was in charge. He was very hard on the rebels. Over 200 rebels were hanged and 800 sold to be slaves in the West Indies. The trials were called the **Bloody Assizes**.

James II makes himself unpopular

James II now allowed Catholics to join the army. This was against the law. James became unpopular. People began to think he was going to make England Catholic again.

James II's elder daughter, Mary, was due to become queen when he died.

People were glad about this because Mary was a Protestant. Her husband, William of Orange, was also a Protestant.

A baby boy arrives

Then, in 1688, James II's wife gave birth to a boy, James. This meant England would be ruled next by a Catholic king, not the Protestant Mary. Some people said the baby was smuggled into the queen's bedroom.

Source D

From a leaflet printed in London in 1679.

Catholic soldiers will attack your wives and daughters. They will hit your children's heads against walls and bash their brains out.

Catholics will steal from your houses and cut your throats.

This is what happened when England was ruled by Catholics before.

Source E

Sir Robert Walpole speaking to the Cabinet.

The Glorious Revolution, 1688

Parliament did not want England to have another Catholic ruler. So it asked William of Orange and Mary to rule England.

William arrived in England from Holland with a big army. He marched to London. James II fled to France.

Parliament had chosen the new king and queen. Historians often refer to this as the **Glorious Revolution**.

New laws

William and Mary were now the Protestant King and Queen. They agreed to new laws.

The new laws meant that Parliament would now have more say in running the country. The power of the King was cut down.

The new laws that cut down the King's power.

No taxation without Parliament's consent

No army in peace time

Freedom of speech for MPs

No Catholic monarch

Parliament to meet at least every 3 years

Queen Anne and George I

Mary died in 1694 and William died in 1702. Queen Anne became the next ruler. She died in 1714 without any children.

James I's great grandson took over. He was George I and he came from Hanover in Germany.

Robert Walpole

Robert Walpole became the first Prime Minister. He led a group of other ministers called the **Cabinet**. The Prime Minister talked to the King about running the country.

Questions

1 Read **New laws**.

   Who had more power after 1688: the King or Parliament?

2 Read **Robert Walpole**.

   Who was Robert Walpole?

The Pale

In 1500 most of Ireland was run by Irish princes.

The Irish people had their own language (**Gaelic**) and their own laws. They were Catholics.

The English ruled some land around Dublin. This land was called the Pale.

Henry VIII (1509–1547) and Ireland

Henry VIII said he was the King of Ireland.

During his reign, England broke away from the Catholic Church.

England became a Protestant country.

Henry VIII wanted Ireland to become Protestant. But the Irish wanted to stay Catholics. They rebelled against Henry.

Elizabeth I (1558–1603) and Ireland

Elizabeth I took land away from the Irish rebels.

She gave their land to Protestant **settlers** from England who went to live in Ireland.

This was called **plantation**. The Irish were very angry about it.

The Irish rebel again

In 1595 the Irish raised an army to fight the English.

Elizabeth I was furious. She sent an army to Ireland.

The fighting was fierce, but the English won.

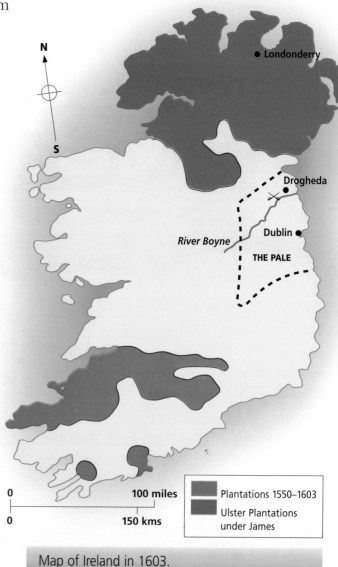

■	Plantations 1550–1603
■	Ulster Plantations under James

Map of Ireland in 1603.

James I (1603–1625) and Ireland

James I did not trust the Irish. He thought they might cause trouble for England.

In 1607 James I sent more Protestant settlers to **Ulster**, the northern part of Ireland.

This was called the **Ulster Plantation**. They took the best farming land away from the Irish.

Cromwell and Drogheda, 1649

In 1641 Irish Catholics rebelled against the English.

They killed thousands of Protestant settlers.

Oliver Cromwell was a Puritan. He did not like Catholics. He wanted to stop the Irish Catholics rebelling.

He went to Ireland with a strong army.

In 1649 he lay siege to the town of Drogheda. But the town would not surrender.

Cromwell's cannon broke through the town walls.

Then his men murdered 3,000 people inside the town. It was a terrible **massacre**.

More land taken

In the 1650s, Cromwell took even more land away from the Irish Catholics.

He sent hundreds of Irish rebels to work as slaves in the West Indies.

Source A

Cromwell said this about the massacre at Drogheda.

Killing lots of Irish people in Drogheda was God's wish. It will stop any more bloodshed in the future.

Source B

This picture of Irish Catholics killing Protestants was drawn in 1641. It made things look worse than they really were.

James II goes to France

In 1688 the Catholic James II fled to France. He was replaced by the Protestant William III and his wife Mary.

James II goes to Ireland

From France, James II went to Ireland. There he helped the Irish Catholics.

He took land from the Protestant settlers and gave it back to the Irish Catholics.

The siege of Londonderry, 1689

Londonderry was a Protestant city. James II raised an army and tried to capture the city.

But the people of Londonderry closed the gates and would not let James in.

James lay siege to the city for sixteen weeks. His army camped outside the city and would not let any food in. He wanted to starve the people into surrender.

William III sends food to Londonderry

William III did not want James to control Ireland. So he sent warships full of food to Londonderry. Source D tells what happened.

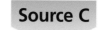
Source C

This painting is on a wall in Londonderry. It was done by a Protestant in the 1980s. William III is shown winning the Battle of the Boyne in 1690.

Source D

The siege of Londonderry, by a person who was inside the city.

James II arrived outside the city on 12 April 1689. We would not surrender to him. His army camped outside the city walls.

During May and June, James attacked the city. One night bombs were put under the walls. Seven people were blown to pieces.

We were short of food. People started to eat horses and dogs. They also drank horses' blood because there was so little water.

Thousands of people starved to death.

In the end we were saved by William III, who sent some warships with food.

The Battle of the Boyne, 1690.

The Battle of the Boyne, 1690

William III was frightened that James II was taking control of Ireland. In 1690 William went to Ireland with an army.

On 1 July 1690, William and James fought a battle at the river Boyne. The fighting went on all day. William won the battle.

James fled from Ireland and went back to France for safety.

After the battle

The English stopped the Catholics from voting or having jobs in the government. Ireland was under the control of English Protestants. It was a conquered land.

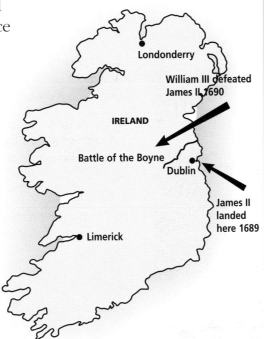

Londonderry

William III defeated
James II 1690

IRELAND

Battle of the Boyne

Dublin

James II
landed
here 1689

Limerick

Questions

1 Read page 72.

   Copy these sentences. Fill in the gaps, using the words in the box.

   Ireland was a ____ country. England was a ____ country. ____ wanted to make Ireland a Protestant country.

   ____ took land from the Irish and gave it to the English. This was called ____.

plantation	Catholic
Henry VIII	Elizabeth I
Protestant	

2 Read page 75.

   What happened at the Battle of the Boyne?

6.2 SCOTLAND AND ENGLAND: A UNION OF KINGDOMS?

Scotland – a separate country

Before 1603 England and Scotland were separate countries. They often fought wars against each other.

Highlanders and Lowlanders

There were two main groups in Scotland:

1 The Highlanders

They lived in northern Scotland and were mostly Catholic. They were divided into big families called **clans**.

2 The Lowlanders

They lived in the south of Scotland. They were mostly Protestant.

James VI and James I

In 1603 King James VI of Scotland became King James I of England. The two countries now shared the same king.

But Scotland still had its own Parliament, law courts and Church.

Cromwell and Scotland

Charles I was executed in 1649. The Scots wanted his son to become Charles II. They gave him an army to fight Cromwell.

In 1651 Charles and the Scots were beaten by Cromwell in the Battle of Worcester. Charles fled to Europe.

Then Cromwell sent an army to Scotland. He closed down the Scottish Parliament and Church. Scotland was now being ruled by the English.

William III and Scotland

In 1688 the Catholic James II was forced to run away to France.

The new king was a Protestant, William III.

The Highlanders hated him. William made the Highlanders sign an oath of loyalty to him. Trouble followed!

The Massacre of Glencoe 1692

The MacDonalds, one of the Highland clans, were six days late in signing the oath of loyalty. That gave William an excuse to punish the Highlanders for being on the side of James II.

In 1692 William sent soldiers to Glencoe, where the MacDonalds lived. The soldiers were friendly for two weeks.

Then one night the soldiers attacked the MacDonalds. The chief and thirty-seven of his clan were murdered. Others ran away across the mountains and died from the cold.

It was an act of terrible cruelty. The Highlanders now hated the English more than ever.

Why did Scotland join with England?

England was much richer than Scotland.

If Scotland joined with England, it could trade with England's **colonies**. This would make the Scots richer.

The Act of Union, 1707

In 1707 Scotland and England joined together. They were now called the **United Kingdom**.

Scotland gave up its own Parliament. Instead it sent forty-five MPs to the British Parliament in London.

It was the Lowland Scots who agreed the Act of Union with England.

The Highlanders did not want to join with England.

Trouble was brewing once again.

The Jacobites

The Highlanders wanted James Edward Stuart as their king. He was the son of James II and a Catholic.

Supporters of James were called **Jacobites** (*Jacobus* is Latin for James).

In 1714 Queen Anne died. The Jacobites thought that James Edward Stuart would be made king.

Instead the throne went to George I of Hanover. The Jacobites were furious.

The Act of Union, 1707

The Scots agreed that:

- there would be one Parliament for the new United Kingdom. It would be held in London.

The English agreed that:

- the Scots could keep their own Church and law courts.

Questions

1 What were the two main groups of people in Scotland?

2 Read **Why did Scotland join with England?**

   Write down a reason why Scotland joined with England.

3 When was the Act of Union?

The Jacobites rebel, 1715

The Jacobites raised an army to put James Edward Stuart on the throne. But they were not very well organised.

The Jacobites were easily beaten in a battle near Stirling. They went back to the mountains. The rebellion was over.

The Jacobites rebel again, 1745

In 1745 James Edward Stuart's son, Charles, landed in Scotland. He was nicknamed 'Bonnie Prince Charlie'.

He said his father was the rightful king. Many Highlanders joined his army.

Bonnie Prince Charlie marches into England

Bonnie Prince Charlie marched into England with an army of 5,000 men. He wanted the English Catholics to join up with him. But very few did.

Bonnie Prince Charlie reached Derby and then turned back to Scotland.

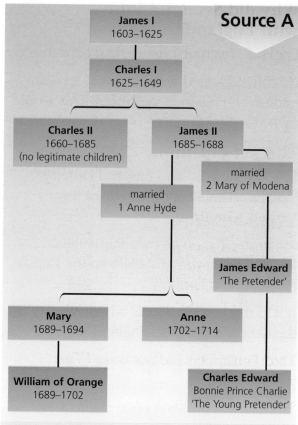

Source A

The family tree of the Stuarts. The dates given are the dates they reigned.

Source B

Bonnie Prince Charlie. He died a drunkard in 1788.

The Battle of Culloden, painted in 1746. The artist was paid by the Duke of Cumberland.

The Battle of Culloden, 1746

Bonnie Prince Charlie and the Jacobites were chased by the English army.

The English were led by the Duke of Cumberland. He caught up with the Jacobites at Culloden in the north of Scotland. The Jacobites were tired, cold and hungry.

There was a bloody battle. The Jacobites were massacred. As the Jacobites ran from the battlefield, Cumberland's men hacked them to death. The Scots nicknamed Cumberland 'The Butcher' because he was so cruel.

Bonnie Prince Charlie escaped to France.

What happened to the Highlanders?

The English sent soldiers to the Highlands so there would not be another rebellion. A lot of Highlanders were driven from their homes. Some went to America.

Scotland gets richer

By 1800 Scotland had grown richer.

Cotton factories were set up in the Lowlands.

Glasgow became a busy port.

Questions

1 Read **The Jacobites** on page 77.

   Who were the Jacobites?

2 Read page 78.

   a In which two years did the Jacobites rebel?
   b Who led the second rebellion?

3 Read **The Battle of Culloden, 1746**.

   What happened in the battle?

Witches

During the 1500s and 1600s, people were very superstitious. They did not know much about science. If something went wrong, people said it was the work of the Devil. People believed that the Devil's work was carried out by **witches**.

What was a witch?

People (usually women) were thought to be witches if they:

- were quite old
- had marks on their bodies
- kept a cat
- lived alone and did not mix
- were poor.

People said that witches got their powers from evil spirits and the Devil.

What were witches supposed to do?

People believed that witches could:

- turn a cow's milk sour
- make horses go lame
- cause storms and make ships sink
- turn children blind.

Doing things like this was called **witchcraft**.

Hunt the witch!

In 1563 Parliament said that witchcraft was against the law. Anyone found guilty of being a witch would be hanged.

Some people became 'official' witch-hunters. The most famous was Matthew Hopkins. He called himself the 'Witch-finder General'. If a woman was thought to be a witch, she was tied up and thrown into a pond. If she floated, she was guilty; if she sank, she was innocent.

Witch hunting ended in the 1750s. By then people did not believe in witches as much.

Source A

Witches standing inside a magic circle. They are swear loyalty to the Devil.

Source B

This vicar did not want Matthew Hopkins in his village.

Every old woman with wrinkles, a hairy lip, a squinting eye and a squeaky voice will be called a witch by him.

Did you know?

Many thought Anne Boleyn, Henry VIII's second wife, was a witch. This was because she had three nipples and an extra finger.

The story of old Mother Osborne

In 1751, Ruth Osborne was accused of being a witch.

Source C

A report in a magazine, April 1751.

At Tring in Hertfordshire, an innkeeper said that Ruth Osborne was a witch.

A mob got hold of Ruth Osborne. She was:

- **stripped naked and her thumbs were tied to her toes**

- **dragged two miles to a muddy stream**

- **ducked in the stream**

- **called names.**

Ruth Osborne choked with mud and died.

The ducking of Ruth Osborne.

Source F

This is what Thomas Colley said before he was hanged.

I murdered Ruth Osborne because I was drunk. I do not believe that there is such a thing as a witch.

Source D

From a letter to the same magazine, June 1751.

Some time ago an old woman called Osborne begged a farmer for some milk.

The farmer said he did not have any milk to give her.

The old woman was angry. She told him the Devil would have his cows.

Afterwards some of his cows became ill. Some stupid people then said Osborne was a witch.

Thomas Colley was arrested for the murder of Ruth Osborne. He was found guilty and hanged in chains.

Questions

1 Read **Witches**.

   Why did people in the 1500s and 1600s believe in witches?

2 Read **What were witches supposed to do?**

   Make a list of things people thought witches could do.

3 Read Source C.

   What happened to Ruth Osborne?

4 Read Source D and Source F.

   Was Ruth really a witch? Explain your answer.

The plague strikes, 1665

The year 1665 was terrible. The plague struck England. It was a horrible illness (see the box below). Over 110,000 people died in London alone.

What people thought caused the plague

People had different ideas about what caused the plague. They said it was caused by:

- dry, warm weather

- poisonous gases

- too many dogs

- God's anger.

Some people even thought that the plague was spread by Jews and Catholics.

The microscope had not been invented in 1665. People did not know that disease was caused by germs in the air.

Prevention and treatment

As people did not know what caused the plague, they had little idea of how to stop it spreading.

They also had few ideas about how to prevent or treat it. Some of their ideas are shown on page 83.

What was 'the plague'?

The main type of plague was called the **bubonic plague**.

The plague was sometimes called the Black Death.

The plague was caused by germs.

These germs were spread by fleas that lived on rats.

The germs were passed on to people if they were bitten by the fleas.

What was it like to have the plague?

Large lumps (called **buboes**) grew under the armpit and in the groin.

These lumps were the size of a chicken's egg.

The lumps were very painful. They turned black and were full of poison.

Then people got a pink rash.

After that, people got a high temperature and a fever.

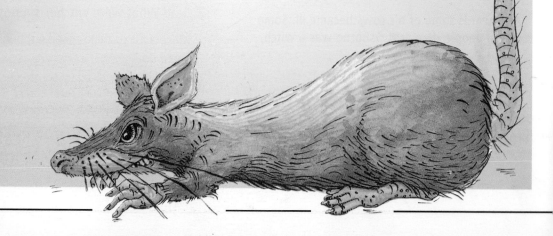

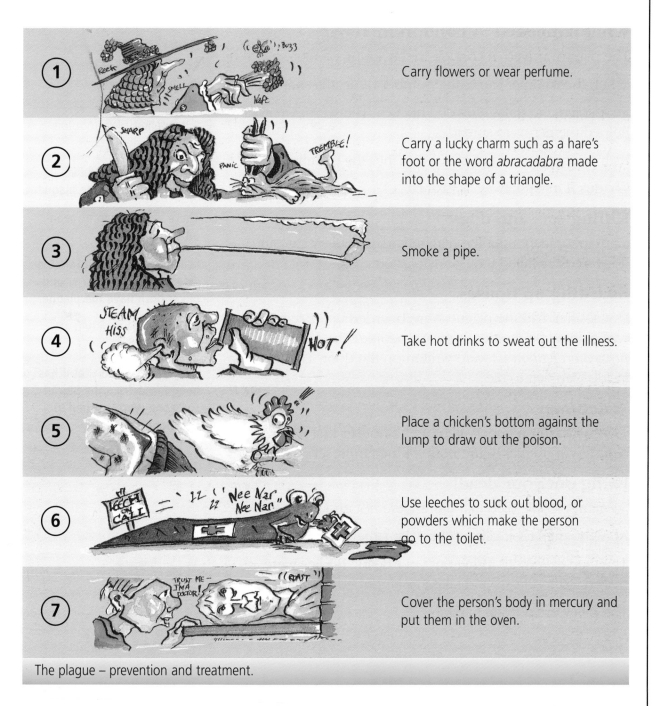

1. Carry flowers or wear perfume.

2. Carry a lucky charm such as a hare's foot or the word *abracadabra* made into the shape of a triangle.

3. Smoke a pipe.

4. Take hot drinks to sweat out the illness.

5. Place a chicken's bottom against the lump to draw out the poison.

6. Use leeches to suck out blood, or powders which make the person go to the toilet.

7. Cover the person's body in mercury and put them in the oven.

The plague – prevention and treatment.

Questions

1 Read **What people thought caused the plague**.

   a What did people think caused the plague?
   b Why didn't they know the real cause?

2 Look at the box on page 82. What was it like to have the plague?

3 Look at the chart above. Do you think any of these ways of stopping the plague helped?

What happened in London in 1665?

The plague arrived in London in the spring of 1665.

When the summer came, the number of deaths shot up.

People lived in dirty, crowded houses. The warm weather helped the germs to spread.

Rich people moved out of London into the countryside.

Charles II moved away to Oxford.

Killing cats and dogs

Many people thought the plague was spread by cats and dogs. So they killed thousands of them.

Boarding up houses

Houses that had the plague were boarded up. A red cross was painted on the door to warn people. The words *Lord, have mercy upon us* were written on the door. The families inside were left to die.

Watchmen

Two **watchmen** kept watch on the houses that were boarded up to make sure none of the family left.

Bring out your dead!

So many people died that there were not enough coffins.

At night, men took carts around the streets of London.

The men called out 'Bring out your dead!' Bodies were put on to these carts and taken to be buried in big pits.

The pits were quickly filled in.

Castleford High School
Technology College
Ferrybridge Road
Castleford
WF10 4JQ

Questions

Read Source A.

1 Write down two things which show that people were scared of the plague.
2 Would you trust what Samuel Pepys says? Explain your answer.

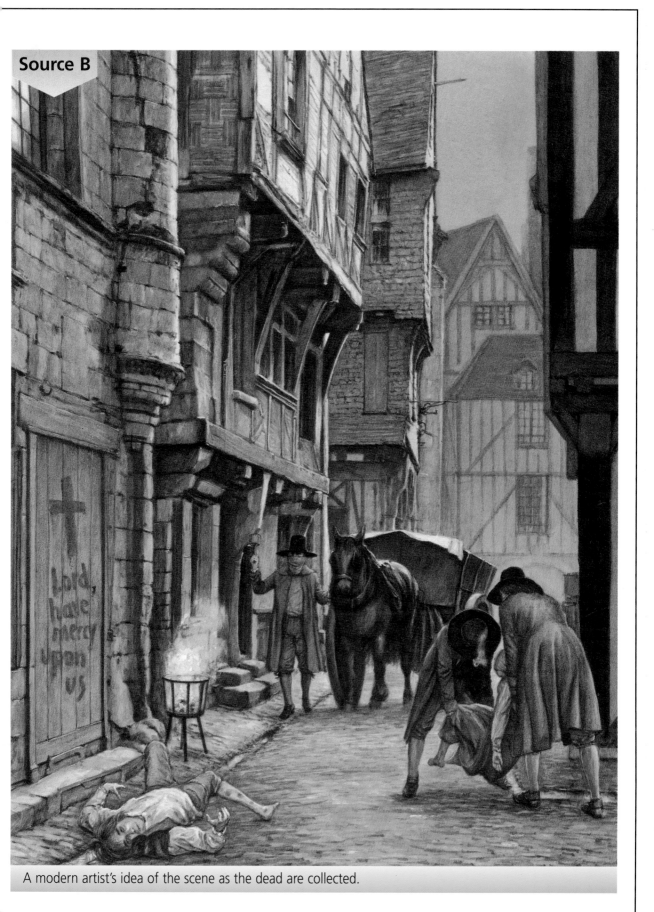

A modern artist's idea of the scene as the dead are collected.

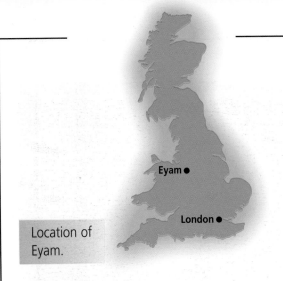

Location of Eyam.

The local people stayed in Eyam. Food was left outside the village for collection. Soon people began to die.

People were scared to go to church, in case they caught the plague from someone else. So William held his services in the open air.

Many deaths

The plague killed 267 of the 350 people who lived in Eyam. One of the last to die was Catherine Mompesson, the vicar's wife.

The villagers, though, had been very brave. They stayed in Eyam, even though they knew they would probably get the plague.

By staying in Eyam, they had not spread the plague to other villages.

The end of the plague

When the cold winter weather came, fewer people died of the plague. The plague was finally ended by the Great Fire of London in 1666. The fire killed the rats, fleas and germs that had brought the plague.

Other places

There were outbreaks of the plague all over England. Ports such as Southampton and Newcastle were badly hit.

Eyam – 'The Plague Village'
George Vicars

Eyam is a small village in Derbyshire. One day in 1665, a parcel of cloth from London was delivered to George Vicars, the local tailor. Within two days, George fell ill and before long he was dead. He had caught the dreaded plague.

William Mompesson

William Mompesson was the Vicar of Eyam. He said no one should leave the village. If people left, they would spread the plague to other places.

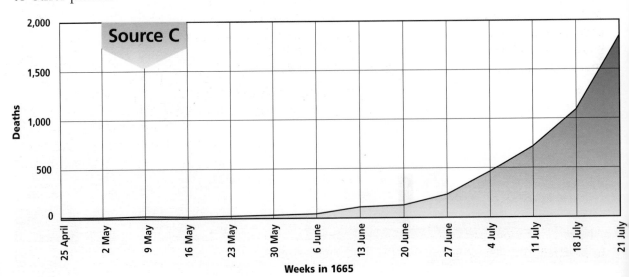

Source C

Weeks in 1665

SAMUEL PEPYS

Samuel Pepys worked for the navy.

Pepys kept a diary. His diary tells us a lot about life in the 1660s.

He tell us about:

- the return of Charles II in 1660

- the plague in 1665

- the Great Fire of London in 1666.

Without Pepys' diary we would not know as much as we do about the 1660s.

Pepys died in 1703.

Source D

Daniel Defoe writing about the plague in 1722.

People would climb out of windows in front of the watchmen.

About twenty watchmen were shot trying to stop people escaping from houses that had been shut [boarded] up.

Deaths in London from April to July 1665.

Questions

1 Read **George Vicars**.

  a Where is Eyam?
  b What happened to George Vicars?

2 Read **William Mompesson**.

  a Who was William?
  b What did he say to the villagers?
  c How did the villagers get their food?

3 Read **Many deaths**.

  a How many people died in Eyam?
  b What was so brave about what they did?

Source A

The Great Fire of London. The artist saw the fire happen.

Fire!

On 2 September 1666, a fire started in a bakery in Pudding Lane, London. It was only a small fire to begin with.

The fire spreads

A strong wind was blowing. The fire suddenly took hold and spread quickly.

The houses were made of wood, so they burned down easily.

There was not much people could do.

The end of the fire

The Great Fire of London lasted for three days. It did a lot of damage. The fire burned down:

- 89 churches
- 13,200 houses
- 400 streets.

Source B

From Samuel Pepys' diary. He lived in London at the time of the fire.

I saw the fire raging.

No one could put it out.

Churches and houses were all on fire.

The flames made an awful noise.

I saw a cat with all the hair burned off its body. But it was still alive!

Who started the fire?

People thought the fire had been started on purpose.
They were sure a foreigner or a Catholic had started it.

Source E

Source C

From Samuel Pepys' diary.

Some people are saying that Catholics started the fire on purpose.
They say Catholics boasted that the hot, dry weather was just right
for starting a fire.

Source D

Written by a modern historian.

In October 1666, Robert Hubert was executed for starting the
fire. Hubert was born in France. He was thought to be a Catholic.
He admitted starting the fire, but later said he was lying. Hubert
arrived in England two days after the fire started. So he could
not have started it!

This column is called the Monument. It was built in 1669 near
to the spot where the fire started. At the bottom it says that
Catholics started the fire.

The Monument was built by Sir Christopher Wren. He also
rebuilt a lot of other buildings, including St Paul's Cathedral.

Source F

A modern historian explains
why the fire was so bad.

The wind was strong.
The water pump near
London Bridge was broken.

The weather had been
very dry. The wells had
no water in them.

Questions

1 Read **Fire!**

   Where did the fire start?

2 Read **The fire spreads** and **The end of the fire**.

   a How much damage did the fire do?
   b Why did the fire do so much damage?

3 Read Source D.

   Why could Robert Hubert **not** have started the fire?

Colonies

Between 1603 and 1750, Britain captured lots of different bits of land across the world. These pieces of land were called **colonies**. All the colonies together made up the **British Empire**.

Trading companies

Trading companies were made up of merchants. Most colonies were started by these trading companies.

The merchants wanted to build up trade and make money.

- From North America they brought furs.
- From the East Indies they brought spices, tea and dyes.
- From the West Indies they brought cotton, tobacco, rum and sugar.

The merchants made money by selling these goods in Britain.

British factories made money by selling cloth, pans, guns and nails to the colonies.

London, Glasgow, Liverpool and Bristol became very busy ports.

Settlers

Many British people went to settle (live) in the new colonies.

Why people went to the colonies

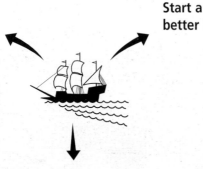

Worship as they liked

Start a better life

Plenty of land to farm

Some colonies gained by Britain, 1655–1713

- Jamaica
- Gibraltar
- Newfoundland
- Nova Scotia
- Hudson's Bay

Source A

A settler tells what America was like in 1620.

The land was empty. There were many wild animals. It was very dangerous.

Source B

Bristol in 1720. The slave trade made Bristol a rich port.

Source C

A cargo ship being built in the East India Company's dockyard on the River Thames.

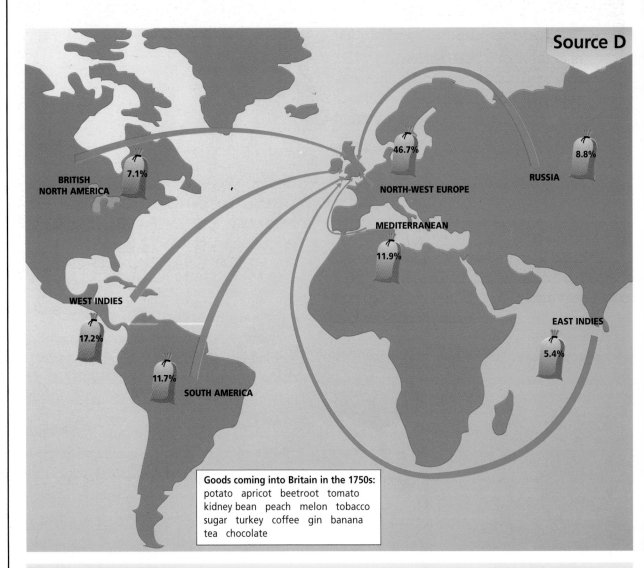

Source D

BRITISH
NORTH AMERICA
7.1%

NORTH-WEST EUROPE
46.7%

RUSSIA
8.8%

MEDITERRANEAN
11.9%

WEST INDIES
17.2%

EAST INDIES
5.4%

SOUTH AMERICA
11.7%

Goods coming into Britain in the 1750s:
potato apricot beetroot tomato
kidney bean peach melon tobacco
sugar turkey coffee gin banana
tea chocolate

In the 1750s, lots of goods were being brought to Britain from all over the world. The percentages show the amount of goods coming from each country.

The slave trade

Some merchants made lots of money out of the cruel slave trade.

How the slave trade worked

1 Ships full of pots, pans and guns sailed to Africa. These goods were traded for black slaves.

2 Then the ships sailed to the West Indies. There, the slaves were traded for rum, sugar, tobacco and cotton. The slaves were made to work in the fields.

Their lives were hard and they often had cruel masters.

3 The ships sailed back to Britain. The rum, sugar, tobacco and cotton was sold.

Sugar fetched very good prices. It was used to sweeten tea, coffee, cakes and puddings.

The slave traders made huge amounts of money. They built themselves big houses to live in.

Source E

A coffee house in London in the 1700s. Merchants and businessmen met here to drink coffee and set up business deals. They also chatted about the news of the day. There were about 600 coffee houses in London.

Source F

An advert in a London newspaper, 1728.

For sale: A black boy, aged eleven. Apply at the Virginia Coffee House in London.

Source G

Written by Daniel Defoe in the 1720s.

Merchants in Bristol trade with places all over the world.

Questions

1 Read **Colonies** on page 90 then write out these sentences, filling in the gaps.

Between _____ and _____ Britain captured bits of land across the world. These pieces of land were called _____.

2 Look at the box on page 90. List three of Britain's colonies.

3 Read **Trading companies** on page 90.

   a What goods did Britain get from:
   • North America   • the East Indies
   • the West Indies?
   b Find these places on the map on page 92.

4 Read page 92.

   Which trade earned lots of money for British merchants?

5 Look at Source E. What can we learn from this source about life in the 1700s?

Source A

The coronation of King Charles II in 1660.

Who was Daniel Defoe?

There were many parts to Daniel Defoe. He was:

- a reporter
- a spy
- a merchant
- a story-teller.

Daniel's childhood

Daniel was born in London in 1660 – the same year that Charles II was made king (see Source A). Daniel's father was a candle merchant called James Foe. He wanted Daniel to be a vicar. But Daniel had other ideas!

Merchant and factory owner

Daniel became a stocking merchant. He travelled all over Europe, but he lost a lot of money. He started up a brick factory. This, too, lost money.

Daniel changes his name

In 1695 Daniel got a job with the government. He changed his surname from Foe to Defoe. Perhaps he thought it was more posh!

Daniel gets into trouble

Daniel now did something very silly.

He started to write leaflets that poked fun at the Church of England. He also wrote bad things about the government.

Daniel was sent to prison for this.

When Daniel came out of prison, he started working as a **spy** for the government.

Source B

A

TOUR

Thro' the whole ISLAND of

GREAT BRITAIN,

Divided into

Circuits *or* Journies.

GIVING

A Particular and Diverting ACCOUNT of Whatever is CURIOUS and worth OBSERVATION, *Viz.*

I. A DESCRIPTION of the Principal Cities and Towns, their Situation, Magnitude, Government, and Commerce.
II. The Customs, Manners, Speech, as also the Exercises, Diversions, and Employment of the People.
III. The Produce and Improvement of the Lands, the Trade, and Manufactures.
IV. The Sea Ports and Fortifications, the Course of Rivers, and the Inland Navigation.
V. The Publick Edifices, Seats, and Palaces of the NOBILITY and GENTRY.

With *Useful* OBSERVATIONS *upon the Whole.*

Particularly fitted for the Reading of such as desire to Travel over the ISLAND.

By a GENTLEMAN.

LONDON:

Printed, and Sold by G. STRAHAN, in *Cornhill.*
W. MEARS, at the *Lamb* without *Temple-Bar.*
R. FRANCKLIN, under *Tom's* Coffee-house, *Covent-Garden.*
S. CHAPMAN, at the *Angel* in *Pall-Mall.*
R. STAGG, in *Westminster-Hall,* and
J. GRAVES, in St. *James's-Street.* MDCCXXIV.

The title page of one of Defoe's books, written in the 1720s.

Daniel the story-teller

In 1704 Daniel started writing story books. His most famous book was about a ship-wrecked sailor called *Robinson Crusoe*.

He also wrote the story of *Moll Flanders*.

Daniel writes about the plague of 1665

In 1722 Daniel wrote a book about the plague of 1665.

Daniel was only five at the time of the plague, so he would not have remembered much about it.

He wrote his book from stories that his uncle had told him.

Daniel writes about Britain

In 1724 Daniel wrote a book called *A Tour Through the Whole Island of Great Britain* (see Source B).

He said he went all around Britain and wrote down what he saw.

But Daniel did not go to all the places that are in the book.

He used information from other people and some that he made up!

Daniel Defoe died in 1731.

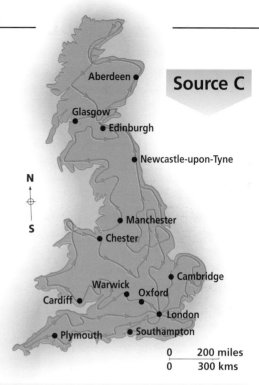

0   200 miles
0   300 kms

Some of the places in Britain that Defoe said he had been to on his 'Tour'.

Source D

What Defoe wrote about Warwick.

The church, town hall and gaol are all new buildings. They are the finest of any town in England.

The George Inn on the corner of the High Street looks like a palace.

There are four horse markets here each year.

Questions

1 Look at Source A. What happened in the same year that Daniel was born?

2 Read **Who was Daniel Defoe?**

   List four things that Daniel did in his life.

3 Read **Daniel the story-teller**.

   Name two famous stories written by Daniel.

4 Read **Daniel writes about Britain**.

   Do you believe what Daniel says Britain was like in 1724? Explain your answer.

Most black people were brought to Britain on slave ships. In 1750 there were about 10,000 black people living in Britain.

Servants to the rich

Rich English people liked to have black people working for them as servants.

It was very fashionable to have black servants.

Black servants did all sorts of jobs. They were:

- pages
- cooks
- coachmen
- maids.

Rich people, such as Elizabeth Dysart, had their portraits painted with black page boys (see Source A).

Rich people took their black servants out to the theatre or for carriage rides.

They thought this made them look fashionable and important.

Many rich people taught their black servants how to read and write.

George I had two black servants called Mustapha and Mahomet.

Source A

Elizabeth Dysart with her black servant. You can read about Elizabeth on pages 66 and 67.

Source B

The port of Liverpool in the 1700s.

Source C

1756 Wanted: A black boy. Must be lively and of good temper.

1757 For sale: Ten bottles of wine, a bottle of cider and a black boy.

1757 For sale: One strong black man, about twenty years of age. Good worker. Also a black boy, about twelve years of age. Good at waiting tables.

1765 To be sold outside St George's Coffee House, a fine black girl. About eight years of age and very healthy.

1768 For sale: A fine black boy. About twelve years of age. Good temper and willing. Speaks English very well.

Black children in Liverpool

Lots of slave ships came into Liverpool.

The ships brought thousands of black children with them to sell as servants.

The black children were sold in shops and coffee houses. People would bid money for them.

The newspapers were full of adverts selling black children.

Rich black children

Not all black children arrived in England to be sold. Some came from rich families in Africa.

Their parents sent them to England to learn to read and write. Then the children went back to Africa and worked in business or as teachers.

Questions

1 Read **Servants to the rich**.

   a Why did rich English people like to have black servants?

   b What jobs did black servants do?

2 Read **Black children in Liverpool**.

   Why were there so many black children in Liverpool?

3 Read **Rich Black children**.

   What other reason was there for black children coming to Britain?

◄ Adverts for buying and selling black children.

UKAWSAW GRONNIOSAW

1 Early life

Ukawsaw was born in Nigeria in Africa. He came from a rich family.

He was taken to America by slave traders.

When his master died, Ukawsaw got his freedom.

He joined the British army. Then, in 1762, he left the army and went to live in England.

2 Life in England

To begin with, Ukawsaw did not get on very well. He was sworn at and had his money stolen.

He married a weaver called Betty. They had three children. They went to live in Colchester.

One winter both of them were out of work. They were given raw carrots by a gardener and money by a lawyer.

Then Ukawsaw got a job in Norwich. But his boss did not always pay his wages. He became poor again. Betty earned some money by weaving cloth.

Then the children caught smallpox. It was a terrible disease and one of the children died. Ukawsaw grew even poorer. He had to sell all his things to pay off his debts.

He moved to Kidderminster. He stayed a poor man and often had to take money from charity.

Ukawsaw did not have an easy life.

Source D

A black trumpeter in the Royal Horse Guards, 1751. There were quite a few black soldiers in the British army.

Source E

An order made by the Lord Mayor of London, 1731.

No black people are to be taken on as apprentices.

A black boy painted in 1732 by William Hogarth. The black boy is wearing jewels and carrying a teapot.

Source F

PHILLIS WHEATLEY

1 Early life

Phillis was a black slave girl.

When she was seven, Phillis was bought by a tailor's wife in Boston, America.

When she grew up, she was very good at writing poetry.

2 Phillis visits England

In 1773 Phillis visited England with her mistress's son.

She met a lot of rich and famous people. They liked her poetry and took her to parties.

Phillis went back to America. Then her mistress died. Phillis had to make a living by selling her poetry.

But she did not make a lot of money.

Phillis died a poor woman in 1784.

Questions

1 Read **Ukawsaw Gronniosaw** and **Phillis Wheatley**.

   Who had a better time in England: Ukawsaw or Phillis? Explain your answer.

2 Look at Source D and Source F.

   What do these sources tell us about England in the 1700s?

What this book is about

This book is about the history of black people in America and the West Indies.

Most black people were taken to America and the West Indies as **slaves**.

Ships full of slaves crossed the Atlantic Ocean. It was a long and very rough journey (look at the map).

Words

Slave: A slave was owned by a master. The slave had to work for the master.

Plantation: A farm that grows cotton, sugar or tobacco.

Most black people came to America from Africa as slaves. This map shows the journey of the slave ships.

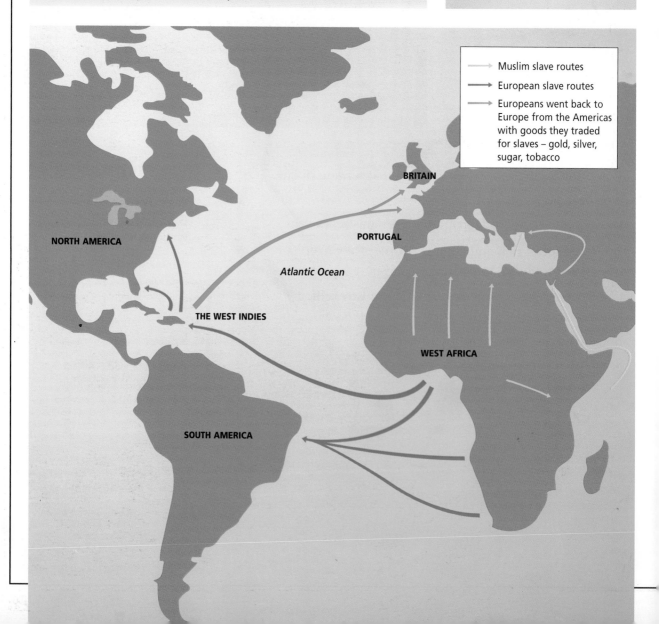

Muslim slave routes

European slave routes

Europeans went back to Europe from the Americas with goods they traded for slaves – gold, silver, sugar, tobacco

BRITAIN

NORTH AMERICA

PORTUGAL

Atlantic Ocean

THE WEST INDIES

WEST AFRICA

SOUTH AMERICA

Hard work and no freedom

Black people from Africa were sold to be slaves in America. They were made to work on **plantations**.

The work was hard. Often the slaves were very badly treated by their masters. Slaves did not have any freedom.

Worse treatment than white people

Slavery was stopped in America in 1865. Black slaves became free people.

Black people thought that they would now have the same rights as white people. They thought they would be equal with white people.

But this did not happen. Black people in America were still badly treated. Often people would not give them jobs just because they were black.

This book is the story of how black Americans have fought to be free and equal. Read on!

Source A

Black slaves working on a plantation in the early 1800s.

What is prejudice?

Prejudice is thinking badly about someone or something, without having a reason to.

The white people in the picture are being prejudiced.

Why white people treated black people badly.

They are not as clever as whites. They need telling what to do, like children.

They are lazy. Without us, they sit around all day.

They are dangerous. Give them half a chance and they will rob you, or worse.

We're just ordinary people. Give us a chance.

Black people left out

The story of the American Wild West has been told mainly by white story-tellers and film-makers. They tell how the 'good' white cowboys fought the 'bad' Indians.

Black people have been left out of the story on purpose. We are left thinking that there were no black people in the West.

Lots of black people

The truth is the opposite! There were lots of black people in the West of America.

There were black cowboys, black farmers, black slaves, black criminals and black miners. Here are the stories of some of them.

Source A

A black American said this in 1926.

If black people are left out of history books, it looks like they are not important.

This map shows the western states of America.

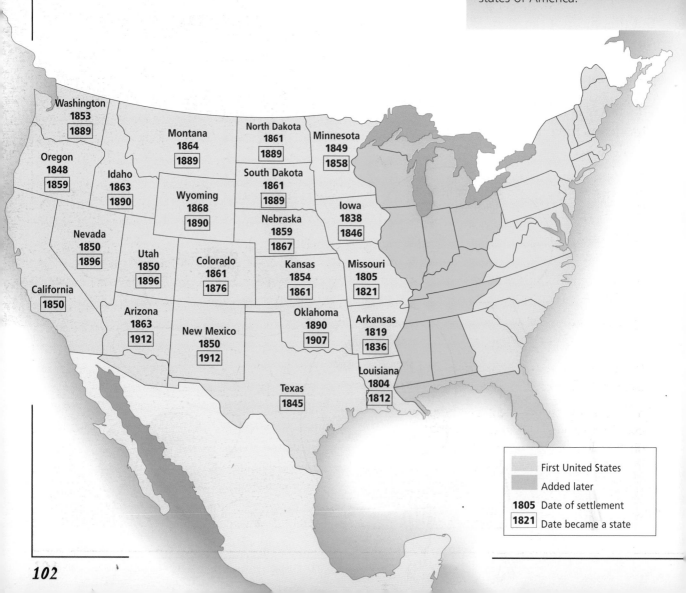

Washington
1853
1889

Oregon
1848
1859

Idaho
1863
1890

Montana
1864
1889

North Dakota
1861
1889

Minnesota
1849
1858

South Dakota
1861
1889

Wyoming
1868
1890

Iowa
1838
1846

Nevada
1850
1896

Utah
1850
1896

Colorado
1861
1876

Nebraska
1859
1867

Kansas
1854
1861

Missouri
1805
1821

California
1850

Arizona
1863
1912

New Mexico
1850
1912

Oklahoma
1890
1907

Arkansas
1819
1836

Louisiana
1804
1812

Texas
1845

First United States
Added later
1805 Date of settlement
1821 Date became a state

Law and order

Some towns had black sheriffs. This man was the sheriff of Abilene, a cattle town in the West. The sheriff kept law and order.

Source B

Black and white miners, digging for gold.

ALVIN COFFEY

Alvin Coffey was a black slave in America.

In 1849 his master took him west to California.

They went to look for gold. A lot of other people went too. It was called the Californian Gold Rush.

Alvin and his master had a long, hard journey to get to California.

When they reached California, they built a log cabin to live in.

They dug for gold. Alvin made $5,000 for his master and $700 for himself.

He was going to buy his freedom, but his master stole his savings.

Alvin had to start saving again. In the end, he saved enough money to buy his freedom.

Black cowboys

Black cowboys were paid the same as white cowboys.

Nat Love was a famous black cowboy. He wrote his life-story.

He said he was treated as an equal by the white cowboys.

When he gave up being a cowboy, he went to work on the railways.

20,000 white cowboys   10,000 black cowboys

The number of black and white cowboys in the West.

Black cowboys were very good at riding and lassooing cattle.

ISOM DART

Some black people in the West broke the law a lot.

Isom Dart was born a slave in 1849.

In 1865 he moved to the West.

He became a cattle thief.

In 1900 Dart was shot dead.

Questions

1 Read **Black people left out** on page 102.

   Why do we not see many black people in films or books about the Wild West?

2 Read about **Alvin Coffey** on page 103.

   Explain how Alvin Coffey got his freedom.

3 Read **Black cowboys** on page 104.

   a How many black cowboys were there?
   b How were black cowboys treated?

4 Look back over pages 103–105. Name a black cattle thief and a kind black woman who lived in the West.

Black women in the West

Black women went west with their families or masters. They sometimes ended up going their own way.

BIDDY MASON

Biddy was a slave. In 1849 she was taken to California by her master. He was looking for gold.

Biddy's master went home after a while. But Biddy and her three daughters stayed. Biddy made some money and bought some land.

Biddy was kind. She gave money away for building schools and churches. She also helped the poor.

Black settlers

When they got their freedom, some black slave families moved to the West. The picture below shows a black family who went to live in the West. Their house is made out of turf. They have two buggies and a wind pump to pump water up from the ground.

MARY FIELDS

Mary was born a slave in the 1830s.

She moved West when she was about fifty years old.

She was a tough woman and had lots of jobs. When she was sixty, she was a stage coach driver! Then she ran a laundry.

One day she was in the saloon. A man did not pay for his drink, so Mary chased him and knocked him out!

Mary died in 1914.

The history of West Africa

Hundreds of years ago, West Africa was split into kingdoms.

There were lots of different **tribes** (groups) of black people.

Craftspeople

The black people of West Africa were clever. They had the skill to make beautiful things out of gold, silver and brass (see Source A and Source B).

Source A

A description of the King of Ghana in 1107.

He has over 200,000 warriors and is very rich.

He is guarded by ten men with gold-handled swords.

Even his dogs have collars made out of gold and silver.

Some early West African kingdoms

Nok	Ife
Ghana	Benin
Mali	Songhai

Some kingdoms and tribes of West Africa in about 1400.

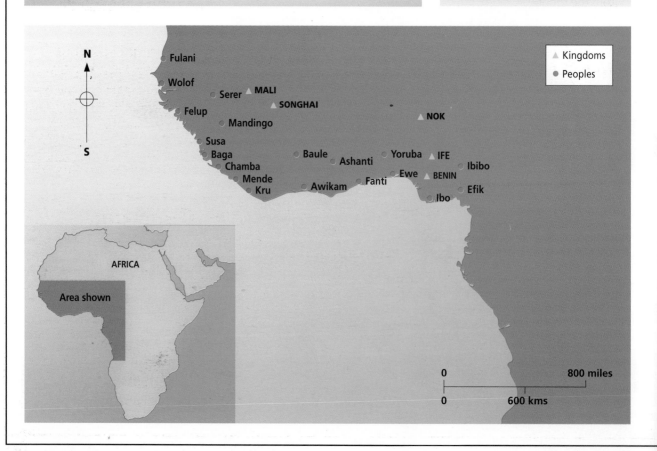

War between kingdoms

The black kingdoms often fought each other. Warriors took prisoners after a battle.

The prisoners were kept as slaves.

Trade with the Arabs

The Arabs lived in North Africa.

They went to West Africa and took salt, spices and books. Then they returned home with gold and slaves.

The Arabs were **Muslims**.

They worshipped Allah. Some black West Africans also became Muslims.

A head made out of brass. It was made in the kingdom of Ife. The people of West Africa were very good at sculptures like this.

Slavery in Africa before white people arrived

White people first arrived in Africa in the 1440s.

There was slavery in Africa before white people came. But it was different from the slavery that came later.

1 Most slaves were captured in battles. Slaves worked for the people who captured them.

2 In some kingdoms, people were made slaves if they broke the law.

3 Some slaves were sold to the Arabs. The Arabs were kind to their slaves.

Questions

1 Read Source A.

   What does the source tell us about this king?

2 Look at Source B.

   What does the source tell us about the black people of Africa?

White people arrive in West Africa

In the 1440s, white sailors from Portugal reached West Africa. They captured black people and took them back to Portugal to be slaves.

Spain, Portugal and America

In the 1490s, sailors from Spain and Portugal landed in America and the West Indies. Settlers from Spain and Portugal went to live there.

The land was empty and wild. There was lots of work to be done. Houses had to be built and farms started. At first, the settlers used white workers from Europe.

Sugar and tobacco

The settlers started to grow sugar and tobacco. Their farms grew bigger, so they needed more workers. They decided to bring black slaves from Africa to work on their farms.

The diagram below shows how black African people ended up in America.

Source A

A model of a white soldier from Europe. It was made out of bronze by a black African.

White settlers went to America.

They grew sugar and tobacco.

There were not enough white workers.

Black slaves were brought from Africa.

Questions

1 Read page 108.

   a When did white people from Spain and Portugal first go to America?

   b Why did they need lots of workers?

   c What did they do to get more workers?

2 Read **England joins in** on page 109.

   Why did lots of English captains start trading in black slaves?

England joins in

In the 1500s, English ships started to take black Africans to America.

Captains realised that there was a lot of money to be made by selling black slaves.

The first English captain to sell black slaves was Sir John Hawkins in 1562.

The slave trade grows

By the late 1700s, many other captains had started dealing in slaves.

In 1771 alone, 92 English ships took nearly 50,000 slaves from Africa to America.

Slavery after 1440

Slavery changed after 1440 when white people got involved.

1 Trading in slaves became a big business. Lots of money was made.

2 Trading in slaves became an overseas trade. It was a long way from Africa to America. Once in America, a black slave would not be able to get back.

3 The treatment of black slaves became very cruel.

Source B

Hans Staden tells how the Spanish treated black slaves. Staden was from Holland. He visited Brazil in the 1540s.

Some Spanish masters are very cruel to their slaves.

They torture the slaves for doing the slightest thing wrong.

Some slaves have run away. When I was in Brazil, I saw slaves rebelling.

A drawing from a book by Hans Staden. It shows slaves being beaten.

Source C

Big business

By the 1700s, the slave trade was big business. Thousands of black slaves were taken from Africa to America. One of them was Olaudah Equiano.

Source A

OLAUDAH EQUIANO

Olaudah was born in West Africa in 1745.

In 1755 he was kidnapped by black people and taken to the coast.

Olaudah was put on a slave ship. He was taken first to the West Indies, then to America.

Between 1756 and 1766 Olaudah was a slave. Then he bought his freedom for £40. He went to England and got married.

In 1777 he started to make speeches in England, saying that slavery was cruel and should be stopped.

In 1789 he wrote his life-story. Many people read it. Olaudah died in 1797.

Olaudah Equiano, painted when he was a free man.

Olaudah's life-story

Here is part of Olaudah's story.

1 Capture

One day my parents were out. I was alone in the house with my sister.

Two men and a woman got into the house and took us away. I called for help, but I was put into a sack. I could not escape. I was taken to the coast. There was a ship waiting to take slaves to the West Indies.

2 On board the ship

The ship's crew had white skin. I had not seen a white person before. The crew pushed me about. I thought they were going to eat me.

There were many other black people on board. They were chained together.

I was so scared that I fainted.

3 Crossing the sea

I was put under the deck. The smell was awful.

People were crying. I was flogged because I would not eat my food.

I did not feel like eating.

I was told that I would be sold to white people in America as a slave.

The smell and heat below the deck got worse. We had to use big tubs to go to the toilet. There was sickness and a lot of black people died.

It was a horrifying journey. I spent some of the time on the top deck. They said I was too young to be in chains. I was lucky.

Source B

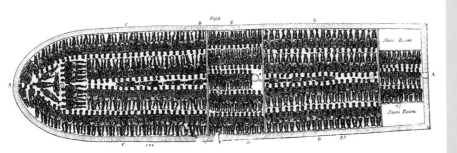

How a slave ship was loaded with slaves. The slaves were packed in very close together. It was very cruel. Conditions were so bad that many slaves died on the journey. The bodies were thrown overboard.

Questions

1 Read the box on page 110. Write down these events in the correct order.

- Olaudah made speeches saying slavery was cruel.
- Olaudah was kidnapped from his village in Africa.
- Olaudah worked as a slave.
- Olaudah wrote his life-story.
- Olaudah bought his freedom.
- Olaudah was taken to America.

2 Can you think why Olaudah Equiano might have thought the white people would eat him?

On arrival the slaves were split up from their family and friends. They were sold to merchants and planters (see Source A).

Once sold, slaves became the property of their master. They had to do as they were told.

Source A

Olaudah Equiano tells of his arrival in the West Indies.

When we arrived, merchants and planters came on to the ship.

They made us jump about to see if we were fit.

The next day we were sold. The buyers rushed to get the slaves they wanted.

Families and friends were split up. They never saw each other again.

What's your name?

Slaves could not keep their own name. They were given a new name when they reached the West Indies. Then, when they were sold, their master often changed their name again. Olaudah Equiano was first called Michael, then Jacob, then Gustavus.

A slave being whipped for breaking the rules. The picture was painted in 1849.

Source B

From person to possession

(1)

Families and friends split up.

(2)

Slaves sold.

(3) "Your name is 'James Jones'."

Slaves named by owner.

(4) "This is James, Anthony. Make him work hard." "Yes, master Jones."

Slaves set against each other by putting some in charge of the rest.

(5) "No talking or singing! No meetings after work!"

Slaves stopped from getting together in groups.

(6) "I've sold you, James. You are 'James Smith' now."

Slave families broken up more than once.

(7) Slaves not allowed to read and write or worship as they want.

Cruel punishments for breaking the rules or running away.

Questions

Read page 112.

1 Who bought the slaves?

2 What happened to families?

3 What happened to the slaves' names?

4 What happened if a slave broke the rules?

What was the war about?

Britain ruled thirteen colonies in America.

By 1776 the colonies had grown tired of British rule. They did not like having to pay taxes to Britain.

The colonies wanted to be **independent** and run their own government.

The colonies started a war against Britain to get their independence.

Source B

A black person said this to the American government in 1791.

You say everyone is equal. Then why do you keep so many black people in slavery?

Source A

From the American Declaration of Independence, 4 July 1776.

All men are equal. God gave all men life, freedom and the right to be happy.

Black people and the war

Some free black people fought against the British.

Some black slaves fought for the British.

The slaves thought they would get their freedom if Britain won the war.

But in 1783 Britain gave up the fight. America was free of Britain.

What would happen to black slaves now?

Source C

A newspaper report of the funeral of men killed fighting against the British in 1770.

Last Thursday, the bodies of Samuel Grey, Samuel Maverick, James Caldwell and Crispus Atticus were buried.

They were killed in the bloody massacre last Monday.

Most of the shops in town were shut and all the bells were rung.

Lots of people came to watch. Everyone was terribly upset.

CRISPUS ATTICUS

In 1770 there was a riot in Boston against the British.

Four Americans were shot dead by British soldiers. It was called the Boston Massacre. One of the men shot was Crispus Atticus. He was a black slave who had run away from his master.

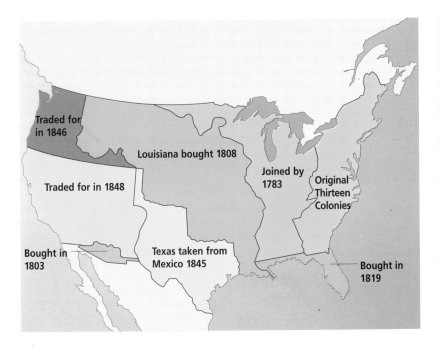

This map shows how the United States grew.

The country was divided into states.

Each state could decide whether to allow slavery or not.

The United States of America

After the war, the thirteen colonies became states. Together they made up the United States of America (USA). Later on, more states joined the USA.

Freedom for slaves?

A **constitution** (list of rules) was written to say how the USA should be run.

The American government had said that all men were equal (see Source A). So black slaves hoped to be set free.

But the new rules said that states could keep slaves if they wanted to.

The southern states grew cotton. Lots of people wanted cotton.

Farmers in the South said it was impossible to grow enough cotton without using slaves. So they kept their slaves.

Source D

The number of slaves in the southern states.

1800	1,000,000
1820	1,500,000
1840	2,500,000
1860	4,000,000

Questions

Read **Freedom for slaves?** and look at Source D.

1 Why did black slaves hope to be freed after the War of Independence?

2 Why did the number of slaves go up in the southern states?

115

The South needed slaves

There was a big demand for cotton. It was taking over from wool as the main type of cloth.

Machines were invented to spin cotton more quickly. Plantation owners in the South said they could not do without slaves.

The North frees slaves

The northern states grew tobacco. But tobacco was becoming less important. So tobacco growers did not need as many slaves.

They let a lot of slaves go free.

Free but not equal

Many black slaves who were freed went to live in northern cities, such as New York.

They found life hard. Many white people were prejudiced. They would not give jobs to black people. Those black people who did have jobs were badly paid.

Black people could not vote. White children had a better education than black children.

Things were far from equal.

Black people might also be kidnapped and sold into slavery. That is what happened to Solomon Northrup (see page 117).

The map shows which states still had slaves in 1860. Are they in the North or the South?

Slave states in 1860
Free states in 1860
Boundary between free and slave states

THE STORY OF SOLOMON NORTHRUP

Solomon was a black person. He was born in New York in 1808.

Solomon's father was a freed slave. He was happy with his wife and children.

Solomon played the violin. One day in 1841, two white men offered him a job in their circus. Solomon took it because the pay was good.

The circus reached Washington. Solomon was having a drink with the two men. They drugged Solomon's drink.

When Solomon woke up, he was chained up and alone in the dark.

Solomon realised he had been kidnapped. The white men beat him up.

Then Solomon was taken to New Orleans and sold into slavery. He was a slave for the next twelve years.

In the end, a lawyer helped him to get his freedom. But he died soon afterwards.

The price of a slave

Slaves varied in price. The price depended on how healthy the slave was, and how badly he or she was needed.

Here are the prices paid by one owner for young male slaves in different years:

1800	$70
1840	$600
1850	$1,500
1860	$2,000

Source A

$1200 TO 1250 DOLLARS! FOR NEGROES!!

THE undersigned wishes to purchase a large lot of NEGROES for the New Orleans market. I will pay $1200 to $1250 for No. 1 young men, and $850 to $1000 for No. 1 young women. In fact I will pay more for likely

NEGROES,

Than any other trader in Kentucky. My office is adjoining the Broadway Hotel, on Broadway, Lexington, Ky., where I or my Agent can always be found.

WM. F. TALBOTT.

LEXINGTON, JULY 2, 1853.

Questions

1 Look at the map on page 116. Name three states that still had slavery in 1860.

2 Read **The North frees slaves**.

Why did the northern states free slaves?

3 Read **Free but not equal**.

Write down two things to show that black people were not treated as equal to white people.

Slaves were in demand in the South. This is an advert for slaves. 'Negro' was the word used for a black person. People don't use it these days because they think it is very insulting.

3.3 SHOULD SLAVERY BE ABOLISHED?

Slaves must be set free

Many people, black and white, said it was wrong to keep slaves. They started to argue that slaves should be set free.

People who wanted slaves to be set free were called **abolitionists**.

Leaflets and speeches

The abolitionists printed leaflets and made speeches.

They also printed a newspaper called the *Liberator*. It was full of stories about black slaves being cruelly treated. Many white people were shocked.

Sojourner Truth (1797–1883)

Sojourner was a black slave, but she ran away from her master.

She was an abolitionist. She went round making speeches about getting slavery banned. She was very famous.

In 1986 the American government issued a stamp with Sojourner on it. This was to remember all she did to get slaves freed.

Abolitionists had different views.

What was said against slavery

Source A

An American preacher said this in 1839.

- Slavery is a curse.

- Slaves are treated like animals.

- Slaves are worked too hard.

- They do not get enough rest.

- Slaves are not well fed.

- They are made to live in bad houses.

- Slaves are made to wear chains and iron collars with prongs.

- Slaves are beaten and then have salt rubbed into the cuts.

- If slaves run away, they are hunted down.

- Then they are whipped and branded, and have their feet chopped off.

What was said in favour of slavery

Source B

The head of a state in the South said this in the 1830s.

- Black people were born to be slaves.

- God meant it to be like this.

- Black people are not as clever as white people. They need to be told what to do.

- Slaves are treated well by their masters.

- If slaves were freed, they would have nowhere to go.

- Slaves eat well and are cheerful.

- They know that their master will always care for them, even when they grow old.

- We need slaves to work on the cotton plantations.

- Without slaves we could not grow so much. We would make less money and be poorer.

Questions

1 Read **Slaves must be set free**.

   Copy and complete this sentence.

   People who wanted slavery stopped were called _____.

2 Read **Leaflets and speeches**.

   What was the *Liberator*?

3 Read **Sojourner Truth**.

   Who was Sojourner Truth?

Fighting quietly on the plantations

Slaves tried to fight for freedom.

Some slaves fought quietly on the plantations. They did this by working slowly. Sometimes they were clumsy. Sometimes they pretended to be sick. They broke the tools or let the animals out. In this way, they worked against slavery. But they did not fight openly.

Running away

Some slaves ran away. This was easier on the West Indian islands. Ex-slaves could live in the mountains or join bands of pirates.

Fighting openly

Sometimes slaves openly fought their owners. But they did not usually win. The white owners banded together to fight against the slaves:

White owners were frightened of slaves fighting to get their freedom. They treated slaves more harshly.

There are some stories of slaves who fought their owners on the next few pages.

Source A

A visitor to a plantation wrote this in 1793.

The slaves are well cared for.

I heard that they were graceful people, but they are very lazy and clumsy.

Question

How did the slaves fight quietly on the plantations?

Find at least two ways.

Slaves harvesting sugar cane in the West Indies in 1823.

Source B

San Domingo

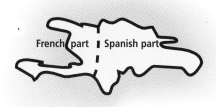

San Domingo was an island in the West Indies.

The French part of San Domingo

Every year 40,000 slaves arrived in ships from Africa.

The white owners worked the slaves to death. It was cheaper to do this, and then buy new slaves from Africa, than it was to look after the slaves properly. French San Domingo had the highest death rate for slaves in all the Americas.

The French Revolution

In 1789 the French people fought against their king. They wanted freedom. The white slave owners in French San Domingo were very worried. They thought their slaves might fight for freedom too.

Boukman leads the slaves

In 1791 a voodoo priest called Boukman led the slaves against their white owners. Boukman and the slaves killed some of the white owners and burnt the plantations. The white owners asked the British for help. The British said yes. They wanted to take over the island themselves.

A new leader – Toussaint L'Ouverture

The slaves found a new leader. His name was Toussaint L'Ouverture. He was captured and died in prison. But the slaves won. They took over French San Domingo and called it Haiti. It was an independent country from 1804.

Source C

A picture made at the time showing the San Domingo slaves fighting their white owners.

Cinque fights for freedom

Cinque was the son of an African chief. In 1839 he was sold to two Spaniards. He and fifty other slaves were put on board a ship. They set off for South America.

The slaves take over the ship

That night the slaves fought the sailors. They took over the ship, and killed the captain and the cook. They put some of the crew in a boat and set it adrift. Then Cinque told the Spaniards to sail the ship to Africa.

Which way did the ship go?

But the Spaniards sailed the ship north to New York without Cinque knowing. Cinque and the other slaves were arrested. Lots of newspapers wrote about their story.

The first trial

The slaves were put on trial. The trial went on for a long time. But at last the jury let the slaves off. There was a lot of argument about it.

The case went to trial again – this time in the Supreme Court. This is the highest court of law in the United States.

The second trial

John Quincy Adams had been President of the United States. He was still a lawyer. He spoke in the Supreme Court on the side of the slaves. He spoke so well that the slaves were set free.

They went back to Africa, where they worked against slavery.

Source D

A picture of Cinque in 1840.

Runaway slaves

The free states in the North did not allow slavery.

Some slaves from the South ran away to the North. They hoped they were safe there. But they were not safe.

The law said that the slaves had to be sent back to their owners in the South.

Courts of law and black people

There were quite a few trials about slavery. Sometimes the slaves won. But often they did not. The case of Dred Scott was bad news for black slaves.

Dred Scott

Dred Scott and his wife and children moved around with their white owner. They spent four years living in free states (states with no slavery). Scott saved up to buy the family's freedom. But his owner said no.

Scott goes to law in 1847

Scott decided to use the money he had saved to go to the law courts. He argued that he had lived in free states, so he had to be free. At the first trial, the court said yes. But the white owner went to another court. That court said no.

Scott goes to the Supreme Court in 1857

Scott went to the Supreme Court. But it turned him down. The Supreme Court said:

Black people are inferior beings who have no rights which the white man is bound to respect.

So Scott and his family were still slaves. They were only set free later.

Why the Dred Scott case was so important

Before the case, it was not clear whether blacks had rights or not. Sometimes blacks did have rights. But here the Supreme Court of the United States said clearly that black people had no rights at all.

Source E

Questions

1 Who was Cinque?

2 What happened to Cinque in 1839?

3 What happened to Cinque and the slaves in the end?

4 Write down what the Supreme Court said in 1857 about the rights of black people.

Some runaway slaves joined Native American Indian tribes. The Native American Indians treated the black people as equals.

The underground railroad was a secret organisation. It helped 75,000 slaves to escape. Many stayed free. About 3,200 black people and white people worked to help the slaves escape.

Slaves tried to escape all the time. They had a much better chance if they had some help.

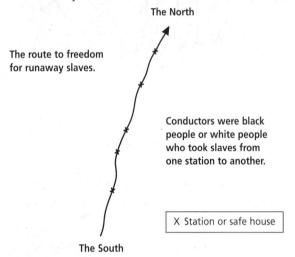

The North

The route to freedom for runaway slaves.

Conductors were black people or white people who took slaves from one station to another.

X Station or safe house

The South

HARRIET TUBMAN

Harriet Tubman was a runaway slave. She was a conductor on the underground railroad. She made about twenty trips. This was very dangerous.

In the American Civil War she worked for the North. She was a spy, a scout and a nurse.

After the war, she worked for women's rights and black rights.

She died in 1913.

John Jones was a brave man. If anyone had found out that he helped runaway slaves, he might have lost his job or even been sent to prison.

JOHN JONES

John Jones was a free black man.

John worked hard as a tailor. He became rich and was respected by both black and white people.

John and his wife hated slavery. Their home was a station on the underground railroad.

They also worked to change the laws for black people in the state of Illinois.

John had several government jobs. In 1874 he won the battle to open all Chicago schools to black and white pupils.

John Jones died in 1879.

Source A

Some slaves went to great lengths to get their freedom. Here is the story of one such slave.

A drawing from the time, showing Henry Brown getting out of the box.

HENRY BROWN

This is a famous escape story.

Henry Brown was a slave. His owner would not buy Henry's wife. So Henry decided to escape.

I decided I would get in a box and be sent through the post to a free state. My friend, Dr Smith, said he would help me. We found someone I could be posted to in a free state.

I got a wooden box made. Then I asked for a few days' holiday so that I would not be missed straight away.

I got into the box with some water. I made a small breathing hole near my face. My friends nailed down the lid of the box and took me to the post office. There were labels on the box to show which way up the box should go.

I started my long journey north. At first they put the box head down, but luckily it fell over. Then it was put on the steamboat head down again. I was left like this for an hour and a half. My eyes were ready to burst from my sockets. The veins on my face swelled. But I made no noise. I was determined to be free or die. Then my box was turned on its side for someone to sit on.

At Washington I was tossed from the wagon. As the box fell, my neck gave a crack and I was knocked out.

I woke up as I was put on another wagon. I was head down again, but soon turned over.

I reached Philadelphia at 3 a.m. At 6 a.m. my box was collected and taken to the address.

People gathered round the box. One of them tapped on it. I said I was all right. They broke open the box and I was free.

Questions

1 What was the underground railroad?

2 What was a station?

3 What did a conductor do?

4 Who was Harriet Tubman?

5 What do you think would have been the hardest thing for Henry Brown during his journey?

3.6 WHAT WAS IT LIKE TO BE A SLAVE?

In the 1930s, the American government collected the life-stories of people who had been slaves.

HENRY TRENTHAM

I was born on Dr Trentham's big plantation. There were about 400 slaves. The slave houses looked like a small town.

There were four overseers. They made us work from sun-up to sunset. Women had to keep up with the men. Most slaves cooked at their houses. We got weekly rations – pretty good, like what you'd have now.

We got a week's holiday over Christmas. We got our shoes for the year. On the Fourth of July, there was a big dinner.

There was a church where the preacher told us to do as we were told. We weren't allowed books, so I can't read or write.

There was a jail for punishment, but not much whipping. The Mistress didn't like the Master to beat us.

MATTIE CURTIS

I was born on a plantation, but me and my family were sold. We were sold on to a preacher. Even though he was a preacher, he hardly fed or clothed his twenty slaves and he whipped them bad.

My job was to mind the slaves' children while they were out in the tobacco fields.

The preacher never paid for us. So we were sold on to Missus Long in Franklin County.

Missus Long was a devil. I worked in her tobacco factory.

Then the Civil War started. She sold us on to someone who was just as bad, if not worse.

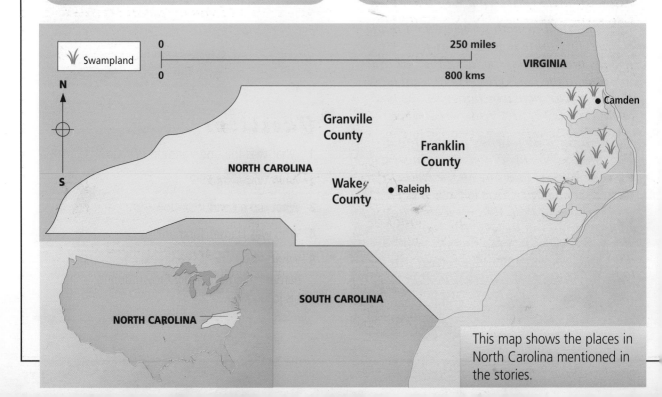

This map shows the places in North Carolina mentioned in the stories.

Five generations of slaves on a South Carolina plantation.

RIA SORRELL

I was born on the Sorrell plantation in Wake County. There were about twenty-five slaves. The Master wouldn't sell us and he didn't believe in whipping. But his wife was a devil. She loved to whip us when the Master was away.

Master Sorrell gave us good houses – two rooms with good beds and enough covers. We had a patch of ground to grow things on.

We had no overseers. The Master just told the oldest slave what he wanted doing.

We got holidays at Christmas, on Sundays and one day a month. He wouldn't allow reading or writing. But he let us go to church.

PATSY MITCHNER

I was born in Raleigh. My master was Alex Gorman, the newspaper man. But he wouldn't let us read or write.

They sold my mother, sister and brother to a slave trader.

Our clothes and sleeping places were bad. The food was real bad. The meat was all fat.

I never saw a slave sold in chains or a jail. I never saw a whipping – whippings were in the back shed.

Questions

1 How many slaves were there on Dr Trentham's plantation?

2 How many slaves were there on the Sorrell plantation?

3 What job did Mattie Curtis do when she was the preacher's slave?

4 Which slave do you think was the luckiest?

The United States

There were a lot of separate states in the USA. In many ways, they ran themselves like small, separate countries. But for big things like having an army or a navy, the states joined together. They made up the United States.

The southern states

In the southern states, slavery was legal. There were many slaves. This was because there were lots of big plantations, growing things like tobacco and cotton. Hundreds of slaves worked on the plantations. The southerners said they could not exist without slaves. They got more and more angry with the northerners, who wanted the South to free all its slaves.

The northern states

In the northern states, slavery was not legal. The northern states did not have big plantations. They did not need slaves. Over the years, they felt more and more strongly that the South should free its slaves.

John Brown

Feelings ran high in the 1850s. John Brown led an uprising of slaves in 1859. He was executed.

Abraham Lincoln elected President

In 1860 Abraham Lincoln was elected President of the United States. He wanted to free the slaves.

But more than anything, he wanted to keep the southern states and the northern states together. He could not do it.

Source A

Sam Houston was the Governor of Texas. He said Texas should not split from the North. It should stay in the Union.

After spending millions of dollars and hundreds of thousands of lives, you may win southern independence. But I doubt it.

The North is determined to keep the Union (United States).

The division of the United States.

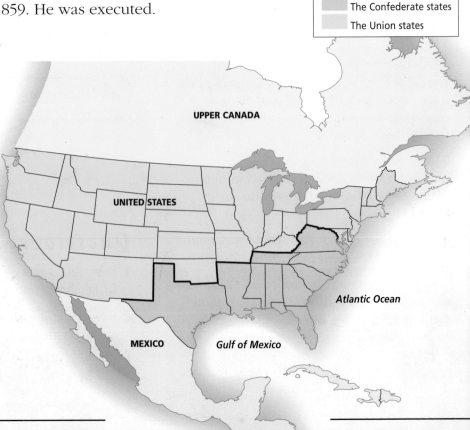

The Confederate states
The Union states

The split – the Confederate States of America

Six weeks after Lincoln was elected, several states left the United States. They set up on their own, and called themselves the Confederate States of America. Lincoln did not know how many more might leave the United States.

The Civil War, 1861–1865

In 1861 war broke out between the United States (the North) and the Confederate States (the South). Many black people rushed to fight for the North. But Lincoln said they could not be soldiers.

He was still hoping for peace with the southern states. He did not want to annoy them by allowing runaway slaves in his army.

But this did not work. There was no peace. The war was the worst that the United States ever fought. Hundreds of thousands of soldiers were killed on both sides.

Slaves set free

In 1863 Lincoln gave the order that all slaves were to be set free. Black people could now join the army.

Many black people fought for the North. But they were paid less money and fought in separate units. They often had white officers.

The end of the war, 1865

The war ended in 1865. The North won, so the slaves in the South were freed. Five days after the war ended, President Lincoln was shot dead.

Questions

1 Where was slavery legal?

2 Write down the names of the two sides in the Civil War.

3 Who became President of the United States in 1860?

4 Which side won the Civil War?

Black soldiers in the Civil War

There were many black slaves in the South. Some slave owners wanted them to fight in the Confederate Army (the South). But the slaves knew that if they did, they would be fighting to keep slavery. Many black slaves ran away to join the Union Army (the North).

ROBERT HOUSTON

After the Yankees (the North) took Memphis, we were told to fight for the Confederate Army (the South). But we ran away.

Then we got taken on by the Union Navy. We got paid $60 a month for two months.

Then I got smallpox, so I was put off the ship on to an island. I cut and sold wood.

Later I was taken off the island and joined the Union Army.

I joined up willingly and have supported the Union all the time.

THE BATTLE OF PORT HUDSON

A white officer writes about his black soldiers.

My soldiers were mostly black slaves who had run away to join the Union Army. I had worries about their bravery. But I have no worries now.

They moved forward under deadly fire. When forced to retreat, they held together and split into groups to fight.

We held our position from 6 a.m. until noon. At 2 p.m. we were ordered to make two charges against enemy guns. The men did not swerve.

I have been in several battles, but never with soldiers of such coolness and daring.

The battle at Port Hudson, May 1863.

Source A

Families of black soldiers

The Union Army did not want the whole family. It just wanted the men. Some men left their families in the South. Other men took their families. The families often lived in camps.

Source B

Families of black soldiers.

MARTHA GLOVER

30 December 1863

My Dear Husband,

I received your kind letter and was pleased to hear from you.

It seems a long time since you left. I have had nothing but trouble since then. I told you how it would be if you went. They beat and insult me, and will not look after me and our children.

The children talk about you all the time. I do not know what will become of me, or them. Do not ask me to beg married men to join the army. I've seen too much trouble.

Farewell dear husband, from your wife,

Martha

Six weeks later, Martha and her three youngest children were sold.

JOSEPH MILLER'S FAMILY

My wife and children came with me when I joined the Union Army in 1864. My master said that if I joined up, he would not look after my family. So they came with me. They had a tent. Then in November my wife was told that they had to leave. My son was sick and they had no place to go.

In the morning, a guard ordered my family out. The weather was very cold. I told the guard that I was a Union soldier and that my son would die. But there was a wagon ready. The guard said they had to get in it, or he would shoot them. They were taken about six miles away.

When I found them that evening, they were cold and had not been fed all day. My boy was dead. But I had to leave them and go back to camp. The next night, I went and buried my own child.

Questions

1 Who were the Yankees – the North or the South?

2 If black slaves ran away to join the Union Army and left their families behind, what might happen?

The Civil War was over. The United States now made three new laws:

1 The Thirteenth Amendment abolished slavery.

2 The Fourteenth Amendment made black people full **citizens**. This meant that they were equal members of the country.

3 The Fifteenth Amendment gave black men equal voting rights with white men.

Did life get a lot better for black people?

Source A

Written by a black writer after the Civil War.

The South was a shambles.

- **Its big cities were gutted.**

- **Its farms were run down.**

- **Its banks were closed.**

About a third of its men had been killed or wounded in the war.

Steps forward

Freedom

Freed slaves could not have their families split up.

- Black people could live where they wanted to.

- They could also take the jobs they wanted.

- Black men could vote, sit on juries and become judges.

Schools

Free schools were set up to help freed slaves to learn to read and write.

Land

Sharecropping was brought in.

Black people farmed the land. Their wage was a share of the crop that they grew.

Black people could now help to make the laws, so that things could get better for them. Hiram Revels is taking up his job as a member of the Senate. The Senate helped to make the laws.

Source B

Steps back

Freedom

Black people in the South found a difference between their legal rights and what they were really allowed to do.

They had the right to vote, but some white people made sure they could not get to vote. They used threats and violence.

Schools

Many schools in the South closed. Some were burnt down.

Land

Sharecroppers had to buy their own tools and other things. Many found that they had to spend more than their share of the crop was worth.

'Jim Crow' laws

The southern states passed laws to keep black people down. These were called 'Jim Crow' laws.

Segregation

Segregation was one way of keeping black people down. Segregation meant separate places for black people and white people.

There were separate places on buses, in churches and in theatres. They had separate public toilets and water fountains.

Going back to Africa

Best for black people

Some black people and some white people thought it would be best for black people to return home to Africa.

Some land was bought in Africa. Some black people went back there. But it never really worked.

Most black people wanted to stay in the United States.

Question

Write out the three new laws after the Civil War – the Thirteenth, Fourteenth and Fifteenth Amendments.

Source C

THE KU KLUX KLAN

This was an extreme group of white people. They dressed up in white robes. They threatened and sometimes killed black people.

Many policemen and judges were members of the Klan. So they often got away with murder.

A Ku Klux Klan meeting.

What happened to the slaves after the war? Here are some of their stories.

MATTIE CURTIS

Right after the war, northern preachers came around to marry all that wanted marrying. They married my mammy and pappy and tried to find their fourteen oldest children, who had been sold on. They only found three of them.

I married Josh Curtis and bought fifteen acres from the land corporation.

I cut the trees and sold the wood and ploughed and planted. Josh helped build the house, and worked on the land. I finally paid for the land, and had nineteen children. Josh and fifteen of the children died. I kept on going.

I'll never forget my first bale of cotton. I was really proud of that bale. I took it to market. White folks hated black folks then, especially if they were making something, so I didn't ask where the market was. I couldn't find it. I went back the next day and asked a policeman. He took me there.

PATSY MITCHNER

When I was about twelve, it was the war. The southern soldiers came through. They stole all they could. Everyone left the Gormans.

I went to Raleigh. I'll tell you, before two years had passed, two out of every three slaves wished they were back with their masters.

Slavery was better for some of us. Had no responsibility, just work, eat, sleep. Slaves prayed for freedom, got it and didn't know what to do with it. Slavery was a bad thing. But the freedom they got, with nothing to live on, that was bad, too.

I've been working for white folks (people), washing and cooking, ever since freedom came.

Source A

HENRY TRENTHAM

After the war, I married Ella Davis. We had six boys and six girls. I think slavery was pretty rough and I'm glad it's all over.

Not all freed slaves became sharecroppers. Some worked for their old owners or did odd jobs..

A preacher visiting a free family in 1881. People could marry and know that their family would not be split up.

Source C

Not everyone wanted to tell their story. This is what Thomas Hall said.

When I think of slavery, it makes me mad.

I don't believe in giving you my story. With all the promises that have been made, the black man is still in a bad way in the United States, no matter what part he lives in.

No matter where you are from, I don't want you to write my story.

The white folks have been, are now and will always be against black folks.

RIA SORRELL

Our soldiers were running away. They took food, animals and even the quilts off the beds. Then the Yankee soldiers came and they took what was left.

When they told us we were free, we stayed with our Master. When the crop was in, the Master gave us part of all we made. We got some meat and crackers too from the Yankees.

After Master died, we moved. I was married by then to Buck Sorrell. We had six children – all but one died. We farmed with the white folks after that, till we got too old to work.

Question

Read about Patsy Mitchner.

What did she say was bad about the freedom slaves got?

By 1880 black people were supposed to have the same rights as white people. But in practice it was very different.

Black people went to their own schools. They lived in a separate part of town. They were much less likely to go to a good school, or to live in a nice part of town.

Say no to segregation?

It was 1898. A black man called Homer Plessy took a railway company to court. He said that they had no right to make him sit in a separate black people's carriage on the train. He said that the American Constitution did not say anything about this. But the Supreme Court (the highest law court in the United States) said that segregation was legal.

How could black people become better off?

The best way for black people to get on was to get a good education. But this was more difficult for black people than for white people. Black teachers were paid less money. Black schools had less equipment. Even so, some black people worked hard to become doctors, lawyers and teachers.

Source A

This college for black students was set up by an escaped slave.

Source B

In 1913, Woodrow Wilson was the first southern President since the Civil War. He was for segregation, and said this:

Slavery did more for black people in 250 years than African freedom has done in a long time. Segregation is not humiliating. It is a good thing.

Organise!

Churches were the first black organisations to help black people. From 1900, other people set up organisations to help black people fight for their rights.

Movement	Aims	Set up
National Negro Business League	To help black businesses	1900
Niagara Movement	To fight for black rights to the vote and equality	1905
National Association for the Advancement of Colored People (NAACP)	To fight for black rights	1909
National Urban League	To help black people who move to the cities to find homes and jobs and to register for government help	1911

These black officers are wearing medals given to them by the French for bravery.

The First World War

The First World War started in 1914. But the United States did not go into the war until 1917. Then many black people joined the army. They worked to get equal rights in the army.

What did the government do about black soldiers?

The government promised to train some black officers. By October 1917 more than 600 black officers had been trained. But they could only join black units.

Black soldiers could not join white units at all. Black men could not join the Marines or become officers in the navy.

War work

Garret A. Morgan, a black scientist, invented the gas mask. Many black people went to work in the factories making things like guns for the war. But white people were worried that black people would take their jobs. Sometimes there was violence.

After the war

Thousands of soldiers came home from the war. They were all looking for jobs. This meant there was more and more bad feeling between white people and black people.

The Ku Klux Klan started up again in the South. In 1919, there were twenty-five riots all over the United States about the colour of people's skin.

Questions

1 Look at the box headed **Organise!**

   a Which were the first black organisations to help black people?

   b What does NAACP stand for?

   c What was the aim of the NAACP?

   d When was the NAACP set up?

2 a What did Homer Plessy do?

   b What did the Supreme Court say?

3 How did black people help in the First World War?

4 Why was there more and more bad feeling between white people and black people after the war?

By the 1920s, black people seemed to be making progress in some ways. But in other ways they were not.

BOOKER T. WASHINGTON

Booker T. Washington was an escaped slave. He set up a college in 1881. It was called the Tuskegee Institute. It was a segregated college and taught mainly practical things like cooking and woodwork.

Some people said this was no good. It just made it seem that black people couldn't do anything more clever.

Booker T. Washington said it was just as good to work with your hands as with your head.

He also said that white people needed time to get used to the idea of black people being good at things.

He was not against segregation.

W.E.B. DU BOIS

W.E.B. Du Bois set up the National Negro (Black) Business League in 1900.

Du Bois was against Booker T. Washington's idea of teaching black people only practical things.

Du Bois said that this just made white people think that black people were not as clever as whites.

Du Bois was well educated himself. He became head of history and economics at Atlanta University.

Du Bois headed the Niagara Movement. This helped black people fight for their rights to have jobs, to worship and to vote. He was also one of the people who set up the NAACP.

Source A

The Ku Klux Klan attacked and sometimes hanged black people. A Niagara Movement meeting in 1906 said:

In the past year, the haters of black people have flourished. Step by step, the defenders of the rights of American citizens have retreated. We want to mix freely with whoever we want. We want the laws enforced against the rich, as well as the poor, white as well as black. We want our children educated.

Source B

Girls at Tuskegee learning how to be maids.

Duke Ellington and his band at the Cotton Club in Harlem.

Harlem

Harlem is an area in New York. It was very famous in the 1920s and 1930s. There were theatres and lots of music of all kinds. Black people composed and performed serious music, musicals and jazz. They wrote books and poetry. White people and black people came to listen to Duke Ellington and Ella Fitzgerald. This showed that black people had real, original talent.

Living in Harlem

Black people felt at home in Harlem. Loften Mitchell grew up there. She said:

It was different from the rest of the city. It was like a small town. Everyone was welcomed and helped to find a home and a job. You might be cooking one thing when a neighbour would drop in with something else and so on, until a family meal turned into a party.

ELTON FAX

Elton Fax moved to Harlem in the 1930s.

I saw Harlem first in the 1930s.

Let me tell you one of the little things that meant so much.

Lacy, a big black policeman, was directing traffic. White folks had to stop and go when he told them. Where I came from, no black person was in charge in that way.

Outside Harlem

Carter Woodson went to Berea College, Kentucky – the only college in the United States that was open to black people as well as white. He set up the Association for the Study of Negro Life and History in 1915.

Dr Hale Williams was black. He was the first doctor to operate successfully on the human heart. By the 1930s, there were many black doctors, scientists and professors.

Questions

1 a Who was Booker T. Washington?
   b What did he do?

2 Why was W.E.B. Du Bois against the ideas of Booker T. Washington?

3 Write three sentences about what Elton Fax saw in Harlem that meant so much to him.

4 Make a list of the ways in which things had got better for black people by the 1930s.

Good times

After the First World War, there were good times. Businesses did well. There were plenty of jobs for everyone.

People thought the good times would last for ever. They spent lots of money and bought **shares** in businesses. Black people did well, though not as well as white people.

Bad times, 1929

All through the 1920s, people went on spending. Share prices went up. But then, in 1929, businesses started to do less well. This meant that share prices went down.

Some people lost all their money. Even banks lost all their money. Suddenly few people had any money, so hardly anyone was buying anything. Many people lost their jobs.

The drought

At the same time, there was a terrible **drought** in the Midwest of the United States. There was no rain. The fields dried out. Farmers lost all their money.

The Depression

The start of the bad times in 1929 and the drought caused what was known as the **Depression**. This went on for several years in the 1930s. As many as 50 million people, black and white, were out of work in the 1930s.

Black people lose their jobs

Before the Depression, there were some jobs that only black people would do. These were jobs like sweeping the streets. But in the Depression, white people were desperate to get any job. Often black people were sacked and their jobs given to white people.

Some families moved to find work. They were called **migrants** (see Source D).

What did the government do to help?

At first, the government did not help. Then, in 1932, President Roosevelt began to help people to find work and get enough to eat.

Source A

FATHER DIVINE

Father Divine was a black church leader. He set up shops to sell cheap food and coal to poor people.

He helped white people as well as black. He also set up restaurants, so that poor people could eat very cheaply or even free.

One of Father Divine's restaurants.

Problems between whites and blacks

Most people were suffering in the Depression. There were fewer jobs and lots of people had no money. White people hit out at black people. There were riots all over the country. In the South, hangings or **lynchings** of black people by white people were common.

JANE MAXWELL

Jane was born in the South in 1916. She began doing housework when she was twelve. She earned $1.50 a week. Then she got married and had a son. But her husband left. Jane worked while her mother looked after the baby. The whole family were often ill.

A friend found Jane work in New York. She worked as a live-in cleaner for $7 a week. She sent for her family. By 1940 she was out of work. But the government paid her $28. Out of this, she had to pay $22 in rent. But she was sure she was better off in New York, and it would be easier to find work there.

Source B

Black farmers talking about farming in the Depression.

If it wasn't the grubs eating the cotton plants, it was the drought. If it wasn't the drought, it was the rains.

What kills us is that we just can't make it here.

Source C

A black farmer from Mississippi (in the South) said it was not true that white people in the North were friendly to black people, while those in the South were not. It was not that simple.

There was a lot of hate in the 1930s. There were riots in the North. We had hate here, too – lynchings. But we went through a lot together. We were all suffering, black and white.

We weren't equal, no question. But we had white friends, white neighbours who'd talk to you, send over food, get you a doctor. I tried Chicago. It was worse up there. No one would even say hello.

Question

1 When did the Depression start?

2 How did the Depression affect black people?

Source D

Black migrant families in the 1920s.

The Depression was a bad time. It was a very bad time for relations between white people and black people.

Some black people began to wonder if it would be better for blacks and whites to live apart.

Go back to Africa?

Some black people wondered whether to go back to Africa. But they had been born in the United States. It was their home.

The Universal Negro Improvement Association (UNIA)

Marcus Garvey founded UNIA. He said:

- that black people should not try to fit into white society
- that black people should be proud of being black
- that black people should look on Africa as their home.

MARCUS GARVEY

Garvey came to the United States from Jamaica in 1916. He set up UNIA. Many people made fun of his ideas. But many ordinary people supported him and gave him money.

Garvey also set up the African Orthodox Church. In its churches, the pictures of God and the holy family showed them as black.

He also set up a shipping line to take black people back to Africa. But the ships were not fit to go to sea.

Garvey was arrested in 1923 and later sent back to Jamaica.

Source A

Marcus Garvey.

Source B

Some of the things Marcus Garvey said.

Black is beautiful.

Up, you mighty people, you can do what you set out to do!

Europe for the Europeans, Asia for the Asiatics and Africa for the Africans.

Question

Look at Source B. Write down the things that Marcus Garvey said.

The Second World War

In 1939 the Second World War broke out. The USA joined in the war in 1941. The war meant there was plenty of work:

1 The army, navy and air force all needed guns, ships and aeroplanes. So there was plenty of work in the factories.

2 The army, navy and air force needed plenty of men to fight.

Black soldiers, sailors and airmen?

Black organisations asked the government to train black soldiers in the same way as whites. They also asked for whites and blacks to work, nurse and fight in the same units.

The government said no

But the government did not think the time had come to treat black and white soldiers in the same way. So it said:

1 Black people could not join the Marines or the Air Corps.

2 Black people could only join the navy to be cooks or waiters, not to fight.

3 The Red Cross stored black people's blood separately from white people's blood.

Things began to change

One black soldier was promoted to be a brigadier-general. In 1941, the army began to train black and white soldiers together. In 1942, the navy and the Marines began to train black troops. The air force started to train black pilots, too.

Source C

Black women working on a train in 1940.

Equality

In 1945, black soldiers and white soldiers fought side by side in the same unit. By this time, over a million black people had joined the forces.

Wartime in the United States

There were plenty of jobs. Black and white people worked alongside each other. But often there were not enough places to live. Then white people could get angry. There were riots in several cities.

Question

1 Why do you think some black people would have liked what Marcus Garvey said?

2 When did black and white soldiers fight side by side in the same unit?

After the Civil War

Many black people moved from the South to the North. Many of them moved to Chicago. This was because it was easy to get to by railway.

Clarksdale, Mississippi

Clarksdale was a small town in Mississippi, in the South. It was surrounded by farmland.

After the Civil War, most of the freed slaves in Clarksdale became sharecroppers or small farmers.

The black people lived on the east side of the railway line. The white people lived on the west side. Black people crossed the line to the white side only if they were going to work for white people.

Chicago

Chicago was a big city in the North. Many black people went there, looking for work and more freedom. But black people were still not treated equally.

Black people lived on the south side of the city and were expected to stay there. They were paid lower wages than white people. They were charged higher rents.

Even so, many black people felt better off in Chicago.

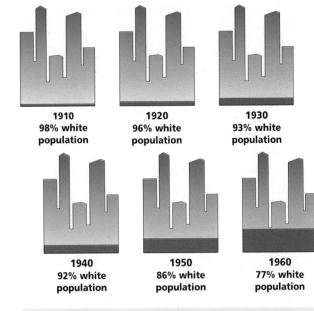

1910
98% white population

1920
96% white population

1930
93% white population

1940
92% white population

1950
86% white population

1960
77% white population

More and more black people moved to Chicago between 1910 and 1960.

Clarksdale

DON'T LOOK ME IN THE FACE

BE HARASSED BY THE POLICE ANYTIME

STAY SEGREGATED

ACCEPT LOWER WAGES AND HARDER WORK

LIVE IN THE WORST HOUSES

GET THE WORST EDUCATION

COOK THE FOOD BUT EAT ON THE STEPS

RISK LYNCHING IF YOU TALK TO A WHITE WOMAN

Chicago

ACCEPT LOWER WAGES AND HARDER WORK

STAY SEGREGATED (BUT WE DON'T CALL IT THAT!)

LIVE IN THE WORST HOUSES

GET THE WORST EDUCATION

How black people were expected to live in Clarksdale and Chicago.

RUBY DANIELS

Ruby was born in 1917. Her father was a sharecropper near Clarksdale.

Marriage

In 1934 Ruby married W.D. Daniels. Four years later, they moved into Clarksdale on a special scheme set up by the government to help people find work. (This was the time of the Depression).

Ruby's work

Ruby worked as a cook for $2.50 a week. If they needed more money, Ruby picked cotton.

In 1940 Ruby's aunt left her husband and moved to Chicago.

Joining the army

In 1941 Ruby's husband joined the army. Ruby found another man. She had two sons.

To Chicago

In 1946 she left the boys with relatives and went to live with her aunt in Chicago. They shared a small flat called a **kitchenette**. Ruby got a cleaning job and earned $40 a week.

In 1954 Ruby's aunt died.

A new man

Ruby started living with a man called Luther Haynes. They had two sons. But finding work was difficult.

Moving and working

They had to move to a flat in a poor part of Chicago. They had a daughter. So by now Ruby had quite a big family. She had a cleaning job and also got some money from the government.

In 1961 they started to buy a house. But Luther started to buy a car as well. They could not keep up the payments. The house went.

A new job and marriage

Then they moved into a tiny flat and started arguing. But things did get better. Luther got a job. They got married in 1962 and moved to a new flat.

A black mother in a Chicago kitchenette in the 1920s.

Source A

Questions

Look at **How black people were expected to live in Clarksdale and Chicago**.

1 Write down the rules that were the same for both places.

2 Which was the worst rule, do you think?

Civil rights

Civil rights are the rights of people to live equally and fairly. In the 1950s and 1960s, more and more black people worked to get civil rights for black people. Some white people joined in, too.

The right to go to a white school

In the South, black children were not allowed to go to white schools. In 1954, a case about this went to the Supreme Court. The Supreme Court said that segregation in schools was illegal. Black and white children were free to go to the same schools.

But some schools in the South ignored this. Often black parents had to go to court. They had to insist that their child should go to a white school. Sometimes that black child was the only one in a school of hundreds of white children.

Cafés and buses

All sorts of places were not open to black people. So they started to protest. They went to white-only cafés or sat on white-only buses.

Non-violence

Some white people in cafés and on buses behaved very badly towards the black people who were protesting. It was difficult for the black protesters not to hit back. But their leaders said that, if they did hit back, they could be thrown out of cafés, buses and other places. So white people got away with beating and threatening black people.

Boycotting

Another way of protesting was **boycotting**. This meant not buying from places that did not give equal rights to black people. There was a famous slogan: *Don't buy where you can't work.*

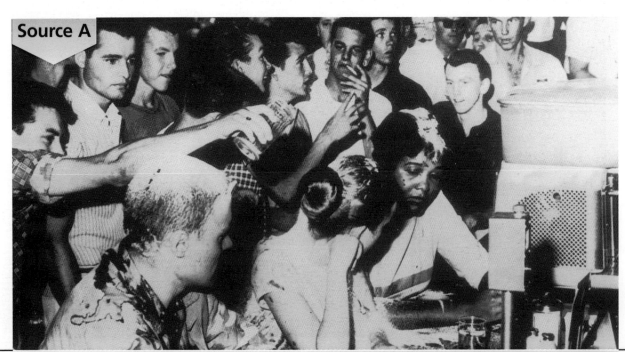

Source A

A black 'sit in' at a white café in Mississippi, 1963

The right to vote

Black people were given the right to vote in 1870.

But many white people in the South stopped black people from going to vote. This went on as late as the 1960s.

FANNIE LOU HAMER

Fannie Lou Hamer was a sharecropper in Mississippi. She decided to register to vote.

On 31 August 1962, I went to the county court house to register to vote.

What happened was that I got home and my children told me the plantation owner, Mr Marlowe, had been looking for me. He arrived soon after and said:

'Fanny Lou, you have been to the courthouse to register. We are not ready for this yet in Mississippi. Take the form back by tomorrow morning, or you will have to leave.'

I was fired that day and have not had a job since. People shot up the houses of black people nearby because of this. Two girls got shot.

Getting arrested

In 1963, I was on a bus when some of the others were arrested for trying to eat in a segregated café. I got out to help, so I was arrested too. They took us to jail. I could hear beating and screaming.

Fanny Lou beaten

Then they came for me. They took me to a cell. There were two black prisoners. They gave one of them a long heavy **blackjack***, made me lie on the other bunk and had him beat me. Then they had the other beat me, while the first one sat on my feet.*

Becoming well known

Fanny Lou became well known. She later said:

If you don't lash back, you can find a real human being in a lot of people.

Questions

1 What are civil rights?

2 What did the Supreme Court say about schools in 1954?

3 a When were black people given the vote?
   b What did many people in the South do about black people voting?

4 Read about Fanny Lou Hamer.

   Why do you think the people whose houses were shot up did not go to the police?

Little Rock, Arkansas, 1957

Little Rock had de-segregated some libraries, parks and even the police force. Then it came to schools.

Nine black children were going to go to a white school. No one was prepared for the way the white people behaved. The white Governor of Arkansas sent in soldiers to keep the black children out. Thousands of people were horrified.

The President of the United States himself overruled the Governor of Arkansas. He said the black children must be allowed to go to the school. In the end, the children were taken into school by government soldiers. The soldiers escorted the black children round the school all day.

This worked while the soldiers were there. But when they left, the white teachers and white children picked on the black children. The nine black children knew that they must not hit back or they would be expelled. One of them was nearly blinded when a chemical was thrown at her.

ERNEST GREEN

I never expected it to be life threatening.

Most people didn't believe that the President would use force to get us into school.

When the troops went, all hell broke loose. They'd taunt you in the corridors, try to trip you, throw ink at you. There were water guns and you'd get phone calls at night, saying they'd have acid in the water guns.

They picked on the girls most. This bunch was really after Minnie. One was like a small dog, snapping at her all the time.

Then he touched Minnie's last nerve. Before I could say 'Minnie don't do it', she had dumped her bowl of chilli on his head. The school board expelled her. In school, they passed round printed cards saying: 'One down, eight to go.'

Some white kids tried to be friendly, but they really got it. We got through it with a combination of family support and helping each other.

ELIZABETH ECKFORD

Elizabeth went to school. Angry white parents shouted at her. Then an armed guard turned her away. She later said:

Lots of black kids were doing what we did. We couldn't fight back or we'd be expelled. That might mean the end of integration.

Integration means blacks and whites together.

The Children's Crusade, Birmingham, Alabama, 1963

Lots of people worked for civil rights in Birmingham. This work included a Children's Crusade. The black children marched towards the white part of town. They knew they would be arrested. In fact, so many children were arrested that the police ran out of police vans. By 4 p.m. nearly 1,000 children were in jail.

The next day, more children marched. The police brought in fire hoses and dogs. After three days, many people were in jail or hospital. Newspapers and television showed children as young as six being soaked with fire hoses and beaten. Thousands of people saw the pictures and they were horrified. Birmingham, Alabama, was shamed into de-segregating.

Source A

Two accounts of the Children's Crusade.

Audrey Hendricks: I was nine when I marched.

I was arrested.

They took me to a room where five or six white men questioned me. I was scared. I was only little. I was in jail for seven days.

Myrna Carter: On the Sunday march, they were waiting.

The firemen were there with hoses, and the police with dogs on leashes.

The police thought it was funny to let the dogs lunge at us, then pull back. We were scared, but we carried on. When the head of police ordered them to turn the fire hoses on, they didn't, even when he swore.

Source B

Marchers caught by a fire hose.

Questions

1 How many black children were going to go to the school in Little Rock?

2 What did the Governor of Arkansas do?

3 What did the President of the United States do?

4 What shamed Birmingham, Alabama, into de-segregating?

Thousands of people worked to make white people change the way they thought about black people. Here are some of them.

MARTIN LUTHER KING

Martin Luther King was a Baptist minister. He was also a civil rights leader. He made speeches. He got people organised.

Martin Luther King believed in non-violence. He said:

It is important to make changes in the hearts and minds of white people, not to break their bodies.

If you have weapons, take them home. 'He who lives by the sword will die by the sword.' Remember that is what Jesus said.

Martin Luther King won the Nobel Peace Prize in 1964. He was shot dead in 1968. There is now a public holiday in the United States in his honour.

Source A

Myrna Carter heard Martin Luther King speak.

At first, I thought I was going to be afraid, but the fear went.

Dr King's voice had a power like no one else's. He could somehow make you leap without realising that you were leaping.

Source B

The woman in the centre of the picture is Septima Clark. She taught thousands of black people to read and write, so that they could vote in elections.

Government troops helped some black movements in the South. But they were not helping here.

ARLEN CARR

First day at school

When I started at Lanter High School, there were thirteen of us. We were all in separate classes. The head teacher opened the door and said to my teacher: 'He's in your class.' The kids saw me. You could have heard a pin drop.

Like a king

I'll never forget how you could be walking down the hall, and they'd just part. The first time, I was a little afraid, but then I felt like a king.

Some friends

After a while, their attitude was 'Well they're here, we've got to accept them.' We did make some friends, mostly from the air force base, where the kids had lived in different parts of the country. They'd been around black kids more.

The last year

In the last year, I asked a white friend to sign my year book. He wrote that he had hated black people. Now he realised that people were people, black and white.

Questions

1 Who was Martin Luther King?

2 Write down what Martin Luther King said about changing white people's hearts and minds.

3 What did Martin Luther King win in 1964?

4 What happened to him in 1968?

5 Look at Source B. How did Septima Clark change black people's lives?

6 Why did Arlen Carr find it easier to make friends with children from the air force base?

John F. Kennedy

In 1963, Martin Luther King led a huge march to Washington. The President was John F. Kennedy. He said:

The time has come for the nation to keep its promise. Those who do nothing are inviting shame as well as violence.

But little was done. Some black people began to think that non-violence was no use. They must fight back.

MALCOLM X

The X in Malcolm X's name stood for all the names taken from black slaves.

At school, he told his teacher he wanted to be a lawyer. His teacher said: *That's not a job for a nigger.* (He meant a black person.)

From then on, Malcolm said that education just made black people expect too little. He said that black people should be proud to be black. They should look after themselves.

Malcolm X was shot dead in 1965.

Source A

Malcolm X spoke to students in 1965.

How do you think I feel to have to tell you: 'My generation sat around like blocks of wood.'

What did we do? We did nothing.

Don't you make the same mistake. Don't try to be friends with somebody who's depriving you of your rights.

They're your enemies. Fight and you'll get your freedom.

Source B

Julius Lester wrote a book called *Look out Whitey! Black Power's Gonna Get Your Momma!* This summed up lots of white people's fears.

Malcolm X made black people aware and made them want to fight. He did not want to awaken the conscience of America about black rights.

He knew America had no conscience.

Source C

This was a peaceful march in 1965.

The march led to a new law. The law gave the government more power to force states to allow black people to vote.

This was a great victory.

But the next day, marchers in the same place were beaten up by police.

Source D

In 1966, these people lost their home and jobs in Alabama because they had registered to vote. Four days after the picture was taken, the pregnant woman started to have her baby. She was turned away from the white hospital. She bled to death before she reached another hospital.

Riots

It was one thing for the law or the President to say that black people had rights. But the policemen and soldiers who carried out the law were often against black people. Sometimes they beat black people up.

More and more black people became angry. They wanted to fight back.

Martin Luther King said:

Everyone underestimated the amount of rage that black people were feeling.

Things get worse

Black people started to use a new slogan: 'Black Power'.

When marches took place, there was more violence. The newspapers reported the black violence, but they ignored the white violence. Many white people read the newspapers. They were afraid of the black violence. They said that they had always thought black people were like that.

Source E

Martin Luther King said this to the newspapers and television in 1968.

If non-violent people like me don't say what you want, we don't get on the news. Who does? The extremists. By doing this you are showing extremist black leaders as civil rights leaders. And you're making violence the way to get publicity for our cause.

Questions

1 Who was John F. Kennedy?

2 Did John F. Kennedy support black rights?

3 Who was Malcolm X?

4 What did Malcolm X's teacher tell him about being a lawyer?

5 What happened to Malcolm X in 1965?

6 Look at Source D and read the caption.

   a Why did the people in the photograph lose their home and jobs in 1966?

   b What happened four days later?

   c Why did the hospital turn away the woman in the photograph when it could see she needed medical help?

Progress for black people

By the 1960s, many black people had got a good education. They had become lawyers, doctors, business people and mayors of towns. But there was still some way to go.

Riots

In the 1960s, there were many riots. Most of the riots were in big cities. Usually the riots were in the poor areas of big cities.

Why were there riots?

There were three main reasons for the riots:

1 Housing

Black people still lived in the worst housing and went to the worst schools.

2 Voting

Black people could vote by law. But often white people stopped them.

3 Jobs

Black people had the lowest-paid jobs.

Source A

Howard Morris, Director of the National Urban League, went to Newark in 1967.

I was visiting family and friends. About three police cars came round the corner. With no warning, they opened fire. They said there was someone with a gun on the roof. But they were firing at ground level.

My stepfather was killed. My brother was badly wounded.

No matter how well you do, there's still white prejudice. I had two degrees. I work with white people. But I was lumped in with rioters.

I was black.

Troops patrol the streets of Los Angeles after the riots of 1965.

Source B

Source C

Riots in Los Angeles, 1992.

From 1960 to 1992

In 1992, there were riots in Los Angeles and some other big cities. This was because black people still had the worst housing and schools.

Source D

A black woman spoke about the riots in Los Angeles in 1992.

It was pretty scary. All the burning, all the rage.

My kids are young. It was hard to explain why their neighbours were doing this. But then, it's been hard to explain why we have to live like this, too. Rubbish on the streets, homes and schools all beat up and not fixed.

Source E

Jean Carey Bond wrote this in the *New York Times* in 1994.

When my son was a teenager, he was walking home from school when a police car screeched to a halt in front of him.

Four white cops jumped out, guns drawn. They threw him up against a wall, patted him down and grilled him, a gun at his head.

A white classmate was passing and identified him to the cops. There had been a mugging. My son fitted the description of the mugger – meaning my son was black.

Source F

Written by the black politician Ron Brown in 1990.

In 1964 Fannie Lou Hamer fought to get just one seat at the Democratic National Convention. Now I am Chairman of the Party. We've come a long way.

But many blacks live in areas with:

- poor schools
- high crime
- drug abuse
- too few jobs
- too little hope.

A recent study shows that it will be seventy years before black men earn as much as white men in the same job.

Questions

1 Write down the three reasons for riots in the 1960s.

2 Read Source A.
   a Why did the police say they opened fire?
   b What was wrong with what they said?

3 Read Source F.
   What problems do black people still have?

Have things improved for black people in the United States? The last few pages have looked at the very real reasons that black people have to be angry. Here are some reasons to be glad.

Source A

John H. Johnson started his own business in 1942. He published magazines.

- In 1942 I got a loan to start *Negro Digest*.
- In 1945 I started *Ebony*.
- In 1951 I started *Jet*.

Then I started up black fashions and black cosmetics. Today I own the biggest black-based business in America.

Sport

Black sportsmen and women are at the top of many world sports. These include running, basketball, baseball and American football.

SPIKE LEE

Spike Lee is a writer and film maker. He makes films for black people. He said:

Film can influence the way millions of people think.

Source B

One of the most popular children's TV shows in the United States and Britain is *Sister, Sister*. It stars black twins.

Three ways to look at the history of black people in the Americas.

We've come a long way. Black people aren't slaves. We have rights. We can vote and have an education. We have important jobs in all areas of life. There are famous black American film stars, basketball players, writers and politicians.

We've had a huge struggle to get any rights at all. And we've got far more rights on paper than in real life. We're most likely to live in bad housing, go to bad schools, and not get work. We're still struggling against prejudice and fear even now.

We're struggling. But we're getting places. History shows life in America hasn't been fair to black people. It isn't fair now. But we're not going to get equality easily, even though we should. Maybe separation is the answer.

Question

Which of the three speakers above do you agree with most?

GLOSSARY

Making of the United Kingdom (pages 4–99)

anaesthetics drugs to stop a person feeling pain.

Anglican Church the name for the Church of England, which is the official religion of England and which has the monarch as its head.

Barebones Parliament members of Parliament chosen by Oliver Cromwell.

Bloody Assizes the trials of rebels who tried to overthrow King James II.

branded marking a person or animal so that they can be identified later.

British Empire parts of the world that Britain had taken over.

buboes large lumps that grew on parts of the body of someone who had the plague.

bubonic plague disease caused by germs being passed on by fleas via rats to human beings.

Cabinet a group of government ministers, led by the prime minister, who advised the king or queen on how to run the country.

Catholic a member of the Roman Catholic Church whose leader is the Pope.

Christendom parts of the world where the Christian religion was dominant.

clan a group of people with the same family background, often the same family name, and led by a chief, especially in the Scottish Highlands.

colonies land or countries that have been taken over by another country, some of whose people also come to settle there.

Dissenters members of Christian religious groups which have broken away from the main Church.

enclosure a way of farming that breaks up and fences off large fields into smaller ones.

favourite a person who is liked best.

Gaelic the native language of the Irish and Scottish people.

general election when people in a country vote to elect who they want to be their Members of Parliament and which political party they want to govern them.

Glorious Revolution when the Catholic king James II fled England and was replaced by the Protestants Mary II and William III, who ruled the country together.

House of Commons the part of Parliament to which members are elected to represent the people in making laws and helping to run the country.

House of Lords the part of Parliament whose members are not elected but who give advice and agree the laws.

Humours parts of the body that were affected in certain ways if you were ill.

Jacobites supporters of the Stuart claim to the British throne.

Lord Protector the person (Oliver Cromwell) chosen to rule England.

massacre the killing of many people.

Members of Parliament (MPs) rich men who met in the Houses of Parliament in London to talk about what the king or queen should do in ruling the country.

Pilgrim Fathers members of the Puritan religious group who sailed to America on the *Mayflower* to start a new life.

priestholes secret rooms in Catholic houses where Catholic priests could hide to escape their enemies.

Protestant member of a Christian Church opposed to the Roman Catholic Church.

Puritans those who wanted the Church of England to be purer and simpler.

republic a country that has no king or queen and is run by people who are elected to parliament.

Restoration when a monarch is returned to the throne of a country.

Rump Parliament Members of Parliament who were left after some of the other members were removed.

settlers people who have left their own country or place to live in another country or place.

slaves people who were bought and sold by other people to do certain kinds of work.

spy a person who watched and reported on other people (especially for a government).

theatre a place where people can go to see a play performed.

Ulster the northern part of Ireland.

Ulster Plantation the part of northern Ireland settled by Protestants.

United Kingdom formed by the joining together of Scotland and England.

watchmen those who kept watch on houses where people had the plague and stopped anyone who tried to leave.

witchcraft the power to do evil things.

Black Peoples of the Americas (pages 100–157)

abolitionists people in the American South who wanted to put an end to slavery.

blackjack a short leather club with a heavy, leaded end.

boycotting refusing to get involved in doing certain things in order make a point about something you disagree with.

citizens members of a city or country.

constitution a written list of rules setting out the ways in which a country should be governed.

Depression this happens when businesses collapse and millions of people lose their jobs.

drought this occurs when there is no rain for a long time and the so dries up and plants die or cannot grow. This can cause a shortage of food and many people may starve to death.

independent a country or state that has its own government.

integration the mixing of people of different races (usually black a white) who had previously been segregated.

Islam the religion followed by Muslims that everyone should obey the will of God as set out in the Koran, the sacred book of Islam.

lynchings hanging people without giving them a trial, even though they might not have done anything wrong.

migrants people who move from one part of a country to settle in another part.

Muslims people who follow the religion of Islam.

plantation a farm or estate where cash crops such as cotton, sugar and tobacco are grown.

segregation the enforced separation of one group of people from another, particularly black people from white people.

sharecropping where a tenant farmer pays his rent by giving the landlord part of his crop instead of money.

shares a way of investing money in a company, so that you own p of that company.

slave a person owned by another person who is the master. The sla has to work for the master.

tribe a group of people who share the same race and culture.

INDEX